Praise for
It's Okay to Cry

"Open the mind of a child and you might expect to find flowers, sunshine, and Sponge Bob. Norm Wright helps us to understand that a child's world is also filled with real hurts and disappointments due to a variety of losses suffered and stored. And, after all, as Charles Dodgson (a.k.a. Lewis Carroll) so eloquently reminds us of adults, 'We are but older children, dear, who fret to find our bedtime near.' The losses of a child's world become the losses of our own psyches. *It's Okay to Cry* was more than a learning experience. It was necessary therapy."

  —MIKE KLUMPP, author of *The Single Dad's Survival Guide*
   and father of eight

"This is a wonderfully helpful, practical book! It needs to be read by every parent, grandparent, and worker with children so we can help a generation that sees too much, is exposed to too much, and consequently knows or experiences too much—too much of everything and often not enough of their parents. This is a book that will help you be there for your child in an understanding and constructive way."

  —KAY ARTHUR, CEO and cofounder of Precept Ministries
   International

"Every parent who has ever said a few words over a goldfish in a toilet bowl or felt the numbness of an unexpected diagnosis in a pediatrician's office will appreciate the heartfelt wisdom in *It's Okay to Cry*. Norm Wright tenderly and skillfully equips parents to help children cultivate a healthy response to life's many pains and sorrows."

  —LORI BORGMAN, columnist and author of *Pass the Faith, Please*

"This is an incredible 'gift' book for all whose lives intersect grieving children. Read it with a highlighter because, sooner or later, you will need the wise counsel that Norm Wright offers. I especially found helpful his suggestions for 'An Anxiety Fable' to help children begin to find words for their losses. I will be a better grief counselor for having read this important, practical resource."

—HAROLD IVAN SMITH, CT, thanatologist and author
of *When a Child You Love Is Grieving*

It's okay to cry

It's okay to cry

A parent's guide to helping children through the losses of life

H. Norman Wright

WATERBROOK

IT'S OKAY TO CRY
PUBLISHED BY WATERBROOK PRESS
2375 Telstar Drive, Suite 160
Colorado Springs, Colorado 80920
A division of Random House, Inc.

Details in some anecdotes and stories have been changed to protect the identities of the persons involved.

ISBN 1-57856-759-9

Library of Congress Cataloging-in-Publication Data
Wright, H. Norman.
   It's okay to cry : a parent's guide to helping children through the losses of life / H. Norman Wright.—
1st ed.
      p. cm.
Includes bibliographical references.
   ISBN 1-57856-759-9
   1. Children—Religious life. 2. Parents—Religious life. 3. Loss (Psychology) in children—Religious aspects—Christianity. I. Title.
   BV4571.3.W75 2004
   248.8'6—dc22

                                        2003026030

Printed in the United States of America
2004—First Edition

10 9 8 7 6 5 4 3 2 1

Contents

When Loss Comes Calling

"I got an empty spot in my tummy. Food doesn't fill it up."
—Susan, age 4

"There's a big hurt in my insides."
—Geniene, age 3

"I don't feel nothing. And I don't want to."
—Jimmy, age 8

"I don't like to play anymore. I have bad thoughts."
—Tom, age 6

"My food doesn't taste good. I don't like to eat."
—Sonya, age 6

"I'm sad all the time. It's like I don't live in my house anymore, but I do."
—Phil, age 7

All of these children have experienced a loss. The particular missing entity may not seem like much of a loss to an adult. But in the life of each child, it was a momentous event. For a child, grief is always about losing something 100 percent; present or future, it's completely taken away.

Will you be able to help a child—your child—through that kind of loss? I know you *want* to. And I believe you'll have the skills to do it after reading this book. But it won't be easy, primarily because it's not an easy thing to move into our painful feelings rather than flee them. In fact, just talking about the topic raises our anxiety levels significantly. I recall several parents discussing their difficulties in talking about death, not just with children, but with anyone. Listen to their comments:

"It makes me anxious. I'd rather avoid it. And I don't want to make others anxious or sad either."

"When I talk about it, I start to cry. I don't like that. Crying can make others cry, and then I feel responsible as well."

"You know, as I think about it, why should any of us know what to say about death? No one I know talks about it."

"I don't want my children to get all morbid. I want them to think about life, not death."

One of our difficulties resides in the fact that children today are sheltered from the normal transitions of life. Death is a stranger, an intruder, not a normal part of living as it was a century or two ago. It used to be that several generations lived in the same house or at least close by. The youngest children learned about birth, illness, old age, and death because these things all happened in their home.

Other generations included children who saw their siblings, cousins, and friends die from diseases such as diphtheria, smallpox, polio, and even the flu. They were around their grandparents so much that they watched them age day by day—and perhaps helped in their care until they died.

And everyone in the family mourned. Together.

Often the local pastor conducted the viewing and funeral in the home. If the body was there for a viewing, it probably stayed overnight. Can you imagine your child (or even yourself, for that matter) sleeping in the same house with a dead body? What used to be so normal would probably be considered "dysfunctional" today.

Many children have never seen chicks born, or puppies or kittens, not to mention a horse or calf. They don't know that some animals are stillborn and never make it. They eat their chicken, turkey, and beef, giving no thought to the fact that *something had to die.*

For other generations, though, death was as much a part of their existence as life. Death happened all around them, so a child grew into the knowledge of death in his own way and his own time. There was less mystery about it.

Yet today our children have become a grief-free generation. We'd prefer to avoid mourning.[1]

In this kind of culture, then, what happens when you or your spouse has an accident, loses a job, suffers a chronic illness, or goes back to school? It's a loss for everyone, including your child. But too often we focus on the adult who is doing the losing or changing. In all the hustle to repair the damage, the youngster stands sad eyed, waiting to be noticed.

And then there's the possibility of a death in the family. None of us wants to believe this will happen until we as parents move into our seventies or eighties and all the children are grown and have families of their own.

Sure, grandparents and great uncles and aunts die; that's to be expected.

But moms, dads, and children do regularly die "before their time." And then the losses multiply, especially for children. And the roles and rules shift dramatically. We'll talk about these things extensively in the chapters ahead. For example, if someone from the immediate family is missing, every family member needs to compensate for that vacancy, including the children:

- *If a mother dies,* it's the loss of the most active caregiver, the keeper of memories, the emotional teacher and guide. Children say:

  "I don't want to think about my mother. It hurts too much to think she won't be around anymore."

  "I got in a fight at school when my friend called me an orphan. I was mad. Mad because he was kinda right. I feel like one sometimes."

  "I dreamed that when I got home from school, my dog was there. When I woke up, I called his name, but he didn't come. I called Mom's name, but she didn't come either!"

- *If a father dies,* it usually means the loss of the major financial contributor as well as the family's "coach." One man was talking to an eight-year-old about the death of his father. The boy, telling us how much he had lost, said:

  "Let me play the piano for you. I know how to play Mozart. My father liked that I could do that. Sometimes he sat with me and turned the pages for me. He would even hum along. He won't do that anymore or hear me again. I like to read. Dad taught me.

I'm learning a computer. Dad was real good on computers. But he can't help me."

- *If a sibling dies,* a child loses out on being the older sibling who teaches or the younger one who is taught:

  "My sister took care of me when I came home. Now the house is empty."

  "We would play music together. I played the piano, and he played the trumpet. Now it just sits in the case. I can hear the sound in my head, but it's just not the same."

In your child's mind, memories of whomever he lost come to the forefront. Some recollections may be good, and some may be bad. The child remembers the sound of his dad's voice when he talked or sang, and that is comforting. But it's also painful, since he won't hear those sounds again. Other children will only recall the shouting or the spankings or maybe only the silence of a dad who was always at work anyway.

Sadly, the good memories will begin to fade, and eventually some will be lost forever. The child won't be able to resurrect them. And this is only one of the additional woundings that come packaged with the initial loss.

WHAT'S THE BASIC APPROACH WITH CHILDREN?

Convinced that loss profoundly affects our children in these ways, we parents determine to help them. But *how?* It has to do with assisting them in the hard work of grieving. If I could sum up the theme of this book in one statement, I'd say: *Grieving our losses is essential to our ongoing emotional health, whether we're adults or children.* I'll let grief-counseling expert J. William Worden expand on this:

> "Is mourning necessary?" I would have to answer this question with a definite, "Yes!" After one sustains a loss, there are certain *tasks of mourning* that must be accomplished for equilibrium to be reestablished and for the process of mourning to be completed.... The adaptation to loss may be seen as involving the four basic tasks outlined below. It is essential that the grieving person accomplish these tasks before mourning can be completed. Incompleted grief tasks can impair further growth and development.
>
> **The Four Tasks of Mourning**
> Task 1: To accept the reality of the loss.
> Task 2: To experience the pain of grief.
> Task 3: To adjust to an environment in which the deceased [or other type of loss] is missing.
> Task 4: To withdraw emotional energy [from the relationship with what has been lost] and reinvest it in another relationship.[2]

As you can see, helping our children "grieve through" their losses is important business for us parents! Children in grief need special attention since they look to their parents for help in navigating the difficult passages of grief. All family members need a balance between being themselves and being a member of the family. On their own, they feel the sharpness of their pain. But then they look to the family for comfort.

Some families or parents overdo and overprotect their children. They think, *Children shouldn't have to go through this!* So they attempt to "fix it" for them. Beware that temptation! We'll delve deeply into this parental ten-dency in a coming chapter, but for now let me remind you: Regardless of the type of loss your family has experienced, the tasks of mourning remain.

Actually, I like to simplify those traditional tasks even further, so you can easily keep them in mind. They are the three steps that will help your children to grieve, and I'll be repeating them throughout this book. Chil-dren need to (1) accept the loss, (2) experience the pain, and (3) express their sorrow.

MORE THAN LITTLE ADULTS—AND *CONFUSED!*

Moving with our children through grief, we can remember what special people they are. As you read through this book, I'll be reminding you about this—especially about how different they are from us adults in their thinking and feeling processes. Developmentally, their brains don't work like ours. Their reasoning is immature, and their understanding of the nature of cause and effect often immerses them in undue pain. One writer on this topic, Joy Johnson, tells an instructive story along these lines:

> I heard the story of one family where a grandmother felt strongly that her daughter's children should not attend their uncle's funeral. She said it wasn't "good" for them and they'd just be "in the way." So the mother complied with her wishes. They stayed with a baby-sitter. After the service they were picked up, and nothing was said about the service. A week later the children began reacting. The three-year-old began disobeying, yelling at his mother and throwing objects. The seven-year-old began wetting the bed and cried a lot.
>
> One day the mother was driving past the cemetery and her three-year-old said, "That's where Uncle Gene is. We can't see him

because we're bad." The mother turned her car around and drove into the cemetery to the uncle's grave. She took the children to the grave and told them they weren't bad. She said she made a mistake not allowing them to attend, and she was going to change that. She met with the funeral director and they had a special service for the children with flowers and balloons. The entire family came to the gravesite for a picnic the next week. All the misbehavior stopped.[3]

Clearly, we can be of much help to our children, our precious little ones who struggle to understand what even adults will never fully comprehend. Worth mentioning here is the sense of confusion that can accompany the loss of a loved one. Just imagine that you are a six-year-old who's been raised in a Christian home, and your mother dies. You will probably wonder...

Where is God?

Why didn't He keep Mommy alive?

Why didn't He make her well?

My uncle told me Mom went to be "up there"!

How high is that?

Why'd God take her so high?

Not only are children confused about God ("If He's so good, why did He take Mom away from us?"), they are also dealing with a swirling mixture of feelings about the person who left ("If Mom really loved me, why didn't she stay here?).

And they're trying to sort through the amazing panoply of mixed messages and so-called words of wisdom they receive from grownups. One adult may be implying: *Oh, you poor little child. You must feel so sad and alone.* At the same time, someone else may be giving the message: *Now you're the man in the family. You'll have to be strong.*

So which is it?

The child's memories of the deceased can also cause confusion. The survivors are talking about this person in a way that conflicts with the child's memories. *Was Mom really as perfect as they say? I didn't know that. Sometimes I didn't even like Mom, and I thought she was bad when she yelled and went on and on... I hope no one finds out what I thought!*

You can see how this would create confusion as well as guilt. In addition, the mood fluctuations of others also generate confusion. Individuals around the child may be cheerful one moment and moody and quiet the next. While this is a normal response, the child is seeking stability and assurance from these people, and their changing moods cause her to question her own responses. She may ask herself, *Is it me? Did I do something wrong? Do they want me around or not?*[4]

WILL YOU OFFER HEALTHY HELP?

Like adults, children need to relinquish and say good-bye to what they have lost. They need to accept the loss, experience the pain, and express their sorrow. They will do this differently than you will, of course. *And they will require your adult assistance*—especially in identifying and expressing the wide range of feelings they're experiencing.

I want to lay the groundwork for the specifics regarding these things (which we'll be exploring in the rest of this book). That groundwork involves raising three "negatives" before we even begin to uncover all the positive results that can flow from grieving and consoling one another in our families. You see, there are some decidedly unhealthy ways families deal with grief. We need to know, and wean ourselves away from, these three seemingly instinctive reactions:

1. It's unhealthy to block emotional expression. Years ago I saw a twenty-five-year-old man in counseling. As we met together, I discovered that his brother, a marine, had been killed seven years earlier. I asked him if he and his brother had been close. His reply was, "Yes, we were *very* close."

I also learned that his mother had turned his brother's room into a shrine by keeping it exactly as it was when he was alive. Nothing had been discarded or changed. I asked this man if he had cried over his brother's death. He responded, "Oh, yes, at his funeral."

Had he visited the grave site? Again he replied, "Yes, at his funeral." But he had neither cried nor been back to the grave for seven years, blocking all emotional expression and grief during that time.

I suggested he take the family picture album, which was filled with pictures of himself and his brother, and visit his brother's grave. He could sit there for a while, reflect on their lives together, pray, and see what might happen. He did so, and when I saw him two weeks later he said, "I went to my brother's grave and did what you suggested. I looked at our pictures and had a lot of memories come back. I prayed and even talked out loud to my brother. It was kind of strange. But after three hours, I cried. Oh, how I cried for him!"

I asked him how this felt, and he said, "It felt...good. It was a long time coming." I wonder how many there are today who need to cry for a brother or sister?

2. It won't help to overprotect. Parents' fearful, overprotective reaction can be harmful to children. Yet it can happen if, for instance, a child has died. The fear of losing another one begins to dominate a parent's thoughts. And the manner in which the first child died may affect the parent's response toward the other children. If the child died of a massive head injury while riding a bicycle, the parents may restrict bike riding to going to and from school or only when accompanied by a parent. And even then, their children must wear double-padded helmets!

A parent's fears can be transferred to the other children as they sense the apprehension in the parent's life. Some children make it a point to prove they will not follow in their dead sibling's footsteps; they become obsessively safety conscious. On the other hand, some become wild and crazy risktakers in order to prove their invulnerability.

3. It's not good to attempt a "replacement plan." Many children who lose a loved one in death (a pet or person) describe it as a "big empty spot" in their life. How will you respond when this is happening in your son or daughter? If you're like most of us, you'll want to fill the void. You'll want to replace that cat or dog or goldfish, or you'll fill your children's lives with toys or gadgets or experiences.

We do seem to prefer such distractions. We don't like to feel empty, and we don't want our precious children to feel empty either. What will this teach them? Think about these messages:

"It's not good or right to feel this way."

"I have to fix this."

"My mom and dad don't think I should feel empty either."

"When I feel this way, my parents think I need something."

"If I need something in the future, I know how to get it."

It's easy for children to override feelings of grief when parents quickly replace the lost things in their lives. Yet this takes them away from the real work, which does include real pain and real loss.

Now that we know of at least three possible unhealthy reactions, we can move forward to pursue the healthy alternatives. That is what we'll do together in the rest of this book. We'll go into much greater detail; we'll explore and expand into many cognate themes. But for now, simply put: *Give uninterrupted time to your children, and listen—truly listen—to their concerns.*

This is valuable not only for your child, but it will also help you shift your focus from the crisis or problem to the normal affairs of life. We all need an occasional break from the crises. Explain the situation to each child (as well as what to expect in the future), according to his or her level of understanding.

Finally, never forget that the "empty spot" in your child's life is actually your child's "teacher." The empty spot is there because of her love for her pet or parent or whatever she lost. Each interaction the little girl misses about her cat teaches her how important Tabby was. It teaches her how much she loved Tabby as well as how much she could love something or someone else. That's good.

In fact, the empty spot is the teacher of every human being. We might even say that there is no such thing as growth—especially *spiritual* growth—without the emptying that comes with loss. I'd like to leave you with that thought as you get ready to launch into the chapters ahead. Loss is not the enemy. It is a painful event, and it is always unwanted.

But it is also a heavenly calling, as we take up the hard work of grieving.

> Come to me, all you who are weary and burdened, and I will give you rest. Take my yoke upon you and learn from me, for I am gentle and humble in heart, and you will find rest for your souls.... Blessed are those who mourn, for they will be comforted. (Matthew 11:28-29; 5:4)

Part I

Knowing the Nature of Loss

Chapter 1

Looking Loss in the Eye

Tears filled Susan's eyes as she looked out the window. There she saw the raggedy legs of her favorite doll…hanging out of the Dumpster. For the brief six years of her life, that doll had been her closest friend. She could hold it, talk to it, and cry with it. But now it was old and smelly. And Mom said it had to be thrown out.

Jimmy didn't understand why all these people were coming to see his mother. Someone said his mother's brother died in a place called the Middle East. But he didn't know this man. He had never met him, though every year the man sent birthday and Christmas presents. Jimmy guessed he would miss those presents.

Janice's closest friend was moving away. For Janice, life stood still. She and her friend had done everything together for seven years. Now Janice was all alone. Her father told her not to be so upset. After all, she'd find a new friend. It was better to have several friends anyway.

Tom was angry. He broke things in his room and yelled at his friends. His dog died two days ago, but his father couldn't understand his reaction. Tom's mother had died three months ago, and Tom didn't show any emotion then. He just sat around as if he were in a fog. Now he was getting upset over a silly dog? It just didn't make much sense.

Do you recognize any of these children? Perhaps you see yourself in one of them. They are all struggling with loss, because loss always begins in our earliest days.

Do you remember the losses of your own childhood? They were there, but perhaps you didn't always identify the searing emotions as a response to loss. Many children don't identify their losses as such. When this happens, they fail to grieve their experiences. To complicate matters, some losses are obvious, others are not. Some are blatant; others are subtle. And some of the experiences involve more than just a loss. They're a crisis—or even a trauma.

No one talks about loss very often. As if by silent conspiracy, we seem to have an unspoken agreement not to raise the issue. We want our children to be winners. Yet with every loss comes the potential for change, growth, new insights, understanding, and refinement—all positive descriptions filled with words of hope.

So how can we help our children get through loss so these potentials might be realized? We can start by looking at the big picture. In this chapter I'd like to offer three broad principles to set the stage for the specific information we'll cover in the coming pages: (1) we can let our children know that loss is normal and unavoidable, (2) we can encourage them to face loss rather than set up unhealthy "protections," and (3) we can prepare ourselves for the task by grieving our own losses in a healthy way.

UNAVOIDABLE, FREQUENT—AND NORMAL

What comes to mind when you think of a loss? Usually it's the death of a loved one. But loss occurs not just through death but by leaving or being left, by staying in one place or moving on. How many death-losses will a person experience in his life? Ten? Perhaps twenty? But other losses can be counted in the hundreds throughout our lives. That's because loss is a normal and unavoidable fixture in our lives as well as our children's.

I like to think in terms of *kinds* and *types* of losses. Let's look at both, in turn.

Some Common "Kinds"

Consider with me some of the most common kinds of losses in the sequence most likely to occur in a child's life. Generally, it's the death of a pet, then the death of a grandparent. Loss continues with a major move, the divorce of the child's parents, the death of a parent, the death of a playmate, friend, or relative. Or there may be a crippling injury to the child or to someone important in the child's life.

This hardly covers the gamut, of course. For example, it's a loss when you're put in an advanced class and your friends stay behind. It's also a loss if your friends are advanced and *you* stay behind! (Which of these did you experience?)

Any move can be a major loss for a child. Can you feel it, even as an adult? Imagine you're a child again, seven years old. Your parents have just moved, and this is your first day at a new school. It's strange and big and scary. You didn't sleep well. Your stomach doesn't feel good, and you have to go to the bathroom a lot. As you walk down the hall to your room, you would rather turn around and run. The door opens and thirty-five strange faces turn around and stare at you. Can you feel it now? For many children a move isn't just a loss. It's a full-blown crisis of aloneness, a feeling of utter abandonment.

A friend saying, "I don't want to play with you anymore" is a loss. Not making the Little League team or simply not getting to play can devastate a child. Not having a favorite dress available for a special day can be devastating for an adolescent girl. Not getting the part in a play can spoil an entire week for some kids.

Sometimes the loss is a case of unexplained withdrawal of involvement by the parents. When Ken was a child, both his parents constantly stayed involved with him in all of his soccer, Little League, and school activities. But when he turned eleven, they not only stopped attending his activities, they didn't even ask him about them. No explanation was given; he couldn't understand it and ached inside for some response on their part. But it never came. This disappointment led to an abiding, unspoken fear: *Maybe everybody will end up doing this to me.* Consequently, Ken developed a sense of caution and suspicion in his life. Years later it showed in his relationships as an adult.

More and more people enter adulthood with a sense of loss because they are children of divorce. *Newsweek* magazine has estimated that 45 percent of all children will live with only one parent at some time before they turn eighteen. The results of studies on children of divorce indicate that the effects are more serious and long-lasting than many parents are willing to admit. And more school-age children will lose a parent to divorce than death. Self-blame for the loss is higher in divorced children than it is in the death of a parent.[1] (You'll learn more about this in a later chapter).

When a family member leaves, it's a major loss for a child. A parent could leave because of a job assignment, a military deployment, separation, divorce, illness, rehabilitation, incarceration, or death. Any of these could lead to a feeling of abandonment.

It's true that some children are physically abandoned, but many more children are emotionally abandoned. Often children don't know why they feel so alone, because their parents never leave them in solitude, and their physical needs are adequately met. But their emotional needs go unmet.

They lack eye contact, hugging, attentive conversation, and emotional intimacy. The verbal affirmations they so desperately need come shrouded in silence. Soon these children begin to think that something is wrong with them, and they carry this perception with them into adulthood. Teenagers are particularly vulnerable because they often seem to want to be left alone, causing parents to withdraw. But the truth is that teens need constant reassurance of their parents' love and attention.

If childhood losses come in multiflavored varieties and are unavoidable, then we should also remember that they will be frequent. Most parents believe their children's losses ought to be few and far between, but it's not true. Even when children seem to escape the major losses, they'll still face frequent loss throughout childhood. Every transition to a new age and stage of development brings both additions and losses, whether it's separation from a parent, home, church, or peer group.

And remember, the everyday losses that aren't resolved can accumulate and create anxiety, depression, and a negative attitude throughout life. The emotions of these childhood losses build up when there's no release, and someday the emotional container will overflow. For all of these reasons, Martha Wakenshaw, in *Caring for Your Grieving Child,* suggests "checking in" with your child each day:

> Starting when my children were about ages three and five, they loved to get into bed and talk about their day, and then ask me to talk about my day. This became a fun ritual for us. Now that my children are of early-elementary age, I check in with them right after school and then again at dinnertime and bedtime.
>
> This is not an interrogation, but a gentle prompting to open the lines of communication. In fact, we make it into a game to say, "I'll tell you one thing I did before lunch, then you can tell me something

you did before lunch." Next I say, "I'll tell you something that happened to me at lunchtime, then you can tell me something that happened to you at lunchtime." Breaking the day into sections can help your child remember the day's events and organize them in his or her mind. [2]

Why is checking in so important? Because loss is a whole-family event. When your child experiences a loss, the family experiences a loss. It affects everyone. When your child experiences a crisis, the family experiences a crisis. And when a child is traumatized, the whole family is traumatized. If the loss in a child's life is a death, the whole family can feel chaotic and out of control. This is predictable and normal.

Another normal response is the feeling that your family will never feel normal or okay again. You will have to create a new normal.

The Typical "Types"

Obviously, this "new normal" accepts loss as a fact of life. So far I've alluded to several kinds of losses, but these actually fall into overarching categories, or types. I'll quickly group and identify at least seven so you can watch for them in your child's experience. As you read through them, think: How have I experienced this type of loss in the past? What is—or will be—my child's experience of it?

1. A material loss. This is a big one for any child. It could involve the loss of a physical object or even familiar surroundings. The greater the attachment, the greater the sense of loss. It's normally the first type of loss for children, or at least one they're aware of. It could be a broken toy or the fact that the dog ate their ice cream cone.

The amount or intensity of loss your child feels is closely tied to the replaceability of whatever he or she lost. When he breaks a favorite piece of sporting equipment or smashes his bicycle, his sense of loss will subside in several days or weeks. But a pet dying has a different impact.

And remember: If the loss is replaceable, the replacement can mask grief. Why? Because parents can immediately provide the apparent solution: "We'll get you a new one."

2. A relationship loss. Here is the end of the opportunity to relate to another person. Kids experience many of these events. When a friend isn't there, you can't talk with her, share experiences, touch, or even argue. This loss can result from a move, a divorce, or a death. It can also arise when having to face cliques in school, not wearing the right clothes, making—or not making—the team, or…just growing up.

3. An intrapsychic loss. That's a fancy word to describe your child's self-perception when she experiences a change. With loss, a child can lose an important emotional image of herself. Not only that, she loses her sense of what she could have become in the future. The loss might force her to change cherished plans or give up a longtime dream.

Often these plans and dreams have never been shared with others, so the loss that occurs is also a secret. Perhaps your son has his heart set on being a star player in Little League—and going on to be a major-league player. But he never learns to hit. Or your daughter wants to be a dancer. And after six years of lessons she shatters her leg. Now the loss involves much more than a throwing arm or a leg; it's intrapsychic as well. The person's vision of who he or she is—and will be—fades into the mist.

4. A functional loss. We're all aware of these, the losses related to a muscular or neurological function of our bodies. They aren't relegated only to the old folks' home; they happen to children, too. If possible, a kid will adapt or adjust, but some functional losses can be absolutely overwhelming.

Here's my own example: When I was nine, I contracted polio. It was a light case, and even though I missed a semester of school, I suffered few aftereffects of the disease. Unfortunately, my doctors felt I shouldn't "overdo," so I wasn't allowed to go out for sports. Fortunately, I put my energies into music and enjoyed some fulfilling experiences in that realm.

5. A role loss. These, too, affect all of us. In a family, it's the loss of a certain accustomed place in the relationship network. It is more or less significant depending upon how much of the person's identity was tied into this role. For example, an only child—starring at the center of family life—suddenly discovers a newborn baby sister sleeping in the room with him. He's no longer the star player. Or what happens when two families attempt to blend and become a stepfamily? With new stepsiblings, each child now faces the task of taking up a transformed role. Since the old role is gone forever, it's a loss.

6. An ambiguous loss. This is a very difficult loss, and it comes in two prickly varieties. In the first type, family members perceive another member as physically absent but psychologically present, because it's unclear whether this person is dead or alive. It's the heartache of the missing soldier or kidnapped child. Will they indeed return someday? Many who lost loved ones in the 9/11 World Trade Center and Pentagon attacks continue to search for a body—or any personal object—that can finally determine the status of an absent loved one. Yet when nothing is available, there is no closure. How can a young child handle this? What if Dad is MIA in Iraq? What if a sibling was lost in a boating accident, but there is no body?

In the second type of ambiguous loss, a person is physically present but psychologically absent. Here is the person with Alzheimer's disease, for example, or maybe a family member has succumbed to addictions, making him numb to the family circumstances. This can happen in the family when children are young. How can they understand what's going on?

Of all the losses experienced in relationships, ambiguous loss is the most devastating because it remains unclear, indeterminate. Perceiving loved ones as present when they are physically gone, or perceiving them as absent when they are physically present, the child begins to feel helpless. Such loss makes any adult or child more prone to depression, fear, anxiety, and ongoing relationship problems. It's not easy for a stepchild to handle the biological parent being excluded. Nor is it easy for a child to constantly deal with a brain-injured dad who now functions like a five-year-old. It all leads to what we know as "complicated grief."

How does ambiguous loss create such problems? First, because the loss is confusing, children are baffled and immobilized. They don't know how to make sense of the situation. And if adults can't cope, how can children deal with it all? They can't problem solve because they do not yet know whether the problem (the loss) is final or temporary.

Second, the uncertainty prevents children from adjusting to the confusion by reorganizing the roles and rules of their relationship with the loved one. Thus the family relationships freeze in place, and children are stuck in what's called a frozen-grief response. This happened with servicemen and their families during the deployment to Afghanistan after the 9/11 terrorist attacks. The uncertainty existed because neither the servicemen nor their families were sure of destinations or return dates. Children would ask, "When is Daddy coming home? Where is he now? How long will he be gone?" But Mommy had nothing to say.

7. A threatened loss. One of the hardest losses of life is the threatened loss. The possibility is real; there is little to do about it. As the possibility looms, the child's sense of control withers away. And for a child, that loss of control hangs over his head like a sword. It's the end of the world for him.

———◆———

In surveying the kinds and types of losses that come into our lives, one thing becomes crystal clear: Nobody likes to lose. When a loss occurs, it must mean that something is wrong...because life is supposed to be filled with winners, right? Therefore, we're tempted to do anything but let our children face the pain. Yes, we try to protect them at all costs. That is the theme we'll take up next.

Chapter 2

Face the Hurt or Try to Protect?

Look at the headlines on your local sports page. All the accolades. The medals. The trophies. They go to winners, not losers, right?

Losing loses out.

Losing hurts. It flies at us with sharpened points that jab into nerves and cause pain. A small loss or a large one—it doesn't matter. It still hurts.

And loss hurts even more because you and I haven't been taught to expect it or shown how best to handle it. Neither have our children. We want to be winners, and we want *them* to be winners. We want success, and we want *them* successful. We want to be in control of our lives, so we build a wall around us with a sign declaring, Losses: No Trespassing! And then, when losses come crashing in, we feel violated.

Yet loss is not the enemy; not facing its existence is. Sadly, many of us have become more proficient in developing denial than in facing and accepting the losses of life. *I don't want this horrible thing happening to my child!* We can't avoid loss or shrug it off though. Even if your child tries to ignore the loss, the emotional experience of it is implanted in his heart and mind. No eraser will remove it.

You see, whenever we have any kind of an attachment, a loss cannot be avoided when the tie is broken. Life is full of relationships with people, things, and dreams that break up—and then new attachments occur. Have you seen this in your child? As each change takes place, *he needs to experience the pain and grief that accompanies it.* But if I, as a parent, don't know how to do this, how can I help someone who doesn't have my adult capability or life experiences to draw upon?

Think of life in this way: It's a blending of loss and gain. Some losses are necessary for normal growth. For instance, your child discovers a tooth that starts to wiggle loose. Soon it either falls out or is pulled. But she'll learn this loss is necessary to make room for the permanent tooth. The child loses a baby tooth but gains a permanent tooth (and sometimes a little money under the pillow), and that's exciting. It pays off. But then big losses occur, some of which may be traumatic. These cause deep pain.

THE GREAT AND HARMFUL TEMPTATION

That pain tempts us to protect in ways that do more harm than good. It's just natural to want to protect our children from the hurt and sorrow of a loss. We parents do this in two main ways.

First, we say: "Don't feel bad. At least you have other friends, toys, grandparents…" At this point we're comparing losses in order to minimize feelings. But a comparison never helps; it does just the opposite. It makes a person (adult or child) in grief feel even worse. The authors of *When Children Grieve* describe it so well:

A loss is experienced at one hundred percent. There is no such thing as half grief. This is particularly true for children. You have all seen a child howl when you take away a toy. The emotional response is immense, and the tears are real. As you begin to apply new ideas to the inevitable losses that occur in your child's life, please remember never to compare losses and never compare or ignore feelings.[1]

Second, parents also tend to edit the story of what has occurred while focusing on anticipated benefits. The hope is that life can remain as normal and pleasant as possible as we help our children "not feel so bad or sad."

"Don't feel bad; this weekend we'll look for a new cat."

"Don't feel bad; it was only a hamster."

"Don't feel bad; Uncle Jerry is in heaven."

"Don't feel bad; he's better off now."

"Don't feel bad; it wasn't your fault."

"Don't feel bad; you'll do better at the next recital."

"Don't feel bad; you did the best you could."

Why is it all right to feel happy when something pleasant happens, but it's not all right to feel sad when something painful occurs? It's been estimated that by the time a child is fifteen years old, he has received more than twenty thousand reinforcements that it's not acceptable to show or talk about sad feelings.[2] Trying to minimize the impact of a loss can leave a child feeling confused, misunderstood, and hesitant to talk about his feelings. And this latter fact is one of the worst things that can happen to a child. My point here is simple: Though loss is normal for children and adults, it is hardly painless; therefore, *we need to see the child's losses through the eyes of the child.*

So, imagine saying things that affirm the legitimate feelings of hurt and sadness. If we were to transform the list above, we might speak along these lines:

"You must be feeling pretty sad right now. You really loved that cat, didn't you?"

"I guess it hurts, losing your hamster like that."

"Feeling sad, huh? Going to miss Uncle Jerry?"

"Seems like you're feeling it: Death is such a sad part of life."

"Feeling guilty about what happened, Tim?"

"I sense that you had high expectations for your performance."

"You did the best you could, and it still hurts. Is that it?"

Of course, you'll use your own well-chosen words within each unique situation. The point is that we can offer an invitation to our children to have and experience all of their appropriate emotions. Shutting down their hurt, anger, and sadness simply buries the emotions for resurfacing later. It also deadens their capacity for true joy.

So keep this in mind: Your child will be most likely to resolve a loss and move on in life if…

- he or she has experienced a secure relationship with the person who has died or left the family for one reason or another. (Even the oldest child leaving for college on the surface generates a loss for the other siblings.)
- he is given immediate and true information concerning the loss. Both allow and encourage the child to ask questions, and then give him answers. Or, if you don't have the information, offer an honest "I don't know."
- she is able to grieve openly—anywhere and anytime—as others do.
- there is another adult available to listen to the child and provide comfort and support over an extended period of time.[3]

When a major loss occurs in the life of your child, it usually means it's the beginning of a series of losses. Whether a child loses a parent to death or separation, the losses continue. For example, the remaining parent may need to work outside the home, work longer hours, and not be available to attend the child's school and sports events anymore. These additional losses may propel the child into a new group at school, with kids who all have only one parent at home.

The oldest child may have to assume more responsibilities at home, creating additional losses of extracurricular school activities. The standard of living probably changes, which will bring another series of losses. After a few years of establishing these changes as a routine (which generates at least some security), the family unit might change again if the remaining parent marries. The children may move into a new home, new school, new church, new friendships, and new routines. And there may be new siblings.[4] And so the losses continue and accumulate.

Keep in mind, however, that there are two sides to losses. The changes that a loss or crisis brings to a family could be for the better. They might actually draw the family closer together as members reevaluate the way they are functioning. They might cause family members to focus on helping one another make positive changes. But too often we find just the opposite occurring. I've seen a loss or crisis fragment the family life and structure. Mom, Dad, and the children become isolated. They try as best they can to rebuild closeness but to no avail.

It's easy for communication lines to become blocked with blame and resentment as part of the process. If conflicts have been simmering under the surface, often loss or crisis brings them bubbling up. So now the family has to deal with the loss as well as the family baggage that just spilled open. At this time the resources to cope may be overwhelmed.[5]

So, although loss is not the enemy, it is a problem. As you continue in this book, you'll find all kinds of practical help to meet this problem. But for now, it's time to look into your own heart and begin taking inventory of your losses and how you've been dealing with them.

So...Have You Faced Your *Own* Hurt?

Take a moment to think about your life as a child. Have you identified the losses there? Do they loom out of proportion to all of your experiences and affect the way you perceive all of your life today? It often happens. We all perceive life from our backlog of experiences, because our memories are always with us. Our perceptions happen automatically, and we believe that what we perceive is actually the real world.

Carefully consider: Who taught you how to handle the losses of life? In our families, we are taught that acquisition, whether of material or non-material things, is the way to be happy and satisfied. We learn to be good in order to acquire attention and praise from our parents and other adults. In school, getting good grades gives us acceptance and approval. Yet teachers and parents rarely teach us how to handle loss, disappointment, and failure.

The drive to acquire continues throughout life, with the advertisers constantly haranguing about what we need to be successful. Thus we grow up with the myth that "acquiring is normal; loss is abnormal." Loss to us feels wrong and unnatural.

It's time to let it be natural. It's time to face loss in ourselves and allow it in our children. It's time to recognize that how we respond to losses today and tomorrow may be the result of how we responded to the early losses in our lives. We begin by soberly asking ourselves the most basic questions, like these:

1. Reflect on one of the earliest significant losses in your life.
   - When and where did this event happen?
   - How old were you?
   - Which people were involved?
   - What are some details of what actually happened?
2. Reflect on your emotional reactions to the loss.
   - What were your feelings at the time?
   - How did you handle those feelings?
   - To what extent did you resolve your sadness, anger, guilt?
   - To what extent is the pain still with you today?
3. Recall any suggestions or advice you received on how to handle the loss.
   - What did your father say?
   - What did your mother say?
   - What did your siblings and other relatives say?
   - What did your friends say?
   - What key statements have stayed with you through the years?
4. What did you learn about loss at an early age that helps you today?

5. What did you learn then that may be hindering the way you cope with loss today?
6. What did you learn that helps or hinders your ability to help your child today?
7. What losses do you expect to experience in the next five to ten years?

The point is this: How do you respond to your own emotions? For many parents, emotions are not only confusing, they're also considered a problem. Many of us were raised emotionally handicapped. We weren't given any real help with our emotional development. And what we don't feel comfortable with, we tend to fear, avoid, or resist. Then we will want to squelch the emotions in our children.

But were you aware that children actually *absorb* emotions? They do. From their earliest days they sense and absorb the emotions of those around them. If you're happy, they pick this up. If you're sad, they do the same. And if you're traumatized, it impacts them—and they watch how you express and process your emotions.

After absorption, the next step is *imitation*. When a loss hits your family and you as a parent begin to grieve, your children will take their cue from what you are doing. If your grief is healthy, so will theirs be. And if it isn't, unfortunately, they will learn that as well.

Often we don't know how to respond to our own feelings, let alone our children's. And it's easy to respond to our children's emotions in such a way that they end up damaged. In his helpful book *The Heart of Parenting*, John Gottman talks about the two hurtful responses of either *dismissing* our children's feelings or *disapproving* of them. If you've ever responded in these ways, don't be alarmed or hard on yourself. It's possible to change. It's important to make the effort to change, though, because parents who dismiss or disapprove tend to treat their children in less than healthy ways.

Dismissing

Parents who dismiss their child's emotions—by ignoring the feelings, disengaging from the child, or ridiculing the way the child feels—are actually saying something about themselves. You see, these reactions are especially likely when the child's emotions are so-called negative ones, because parents often see these reflecting on themselves in some way. They think perhaps it could mean their child is maladjusted or weak. Some go to the extreme of believing any expression of negative emotions indicates bad character traits.

When their child does express emotions, these parents feel uncomfortable, afraid, anxious, bothered, hurt, or even overwhelmed. They're afraid of getting out of control emotionally. Their natural response is, "Let's get past this emotion as quickly as possible."

But suppose they simply try to understand what the emotion *means?* If they don't, they miss a wonderful learning opportunity—and the chance to do some problem solving with their child. They also miss out on the closeness, the intimacy, that is formed when human beings share their deepest feelings.

Disapproving

If parents disapprove of the emotional expression, they are exhibiting a strong, controlling reaction. It is a critical and judgmental parental response.

Instead, when our kids share their emotions, we parents can take a positive cue: *This is a teachable moment.* This is the time to be empathetic, listening with our heart as well as with our head. Help your child put a name to the emotion, give guidance when needed, set limits, and teach acceptable expressions. This is one of your best opportunities to teach your child how to resolve problems.[6]

The following is a an example from Dr. Gottman that describes how to respond to a typical loss for a child:

Imagine, for a moment, a situation where eight-year-old William comes in from the yard, looking dejected because the kids next door have refused to play with him. His dad, Bob, looks up from his paper just long enough to say, "Not again! Look, William, you're a big kid now, not a baby. Don't get upset every time somebody gives you the cold shoulder. Just forget about it. Call one of your buddies from school. Read a book. Watch a little TV."

Because children usually believe their parents' assessments, chances are William's thinking: "Dad's right. I'm acting like a baby, what's wrong with me? Why can't I just forget it like Dad says? I'm such a wimp. Nobody wants to be my friend."

Now imagine how William might feel if his father responds differently when he comes in. What if Dad puts down his newspaper, looks at his son, and says: "You look kind of sad, William. Tell me what's going on."

And if Bob listens—really listens with an open heart—perhaps William will come up with a different assessment of himself. This conversation might continue like this:

William:	"Tom and Patrick won't let me play basketball with them."
Dad:	"I'll bet that hurt your feelings."
William:	"Yeah it did. It made me mad, too."
Dad:	"I can see that."
William:	"There's no reason why I can't shoot baskets with them."
Dad:	"Did you talk to them about it?"
William:	"Nah, I don't want to."
Dad:	"What do you want to do?"
William:	"I don't know. Maybe I'll just blow it off."
Dad:	"You think that's a better idea?"

William: "Yeah, 'cuz they'll probably change their minds tomorrow. I think I'll call one of my friends from school, or read a book. Maybe I'll watch some TV."[7]

There's really no mystery here: *As you learn to handle your own emotions, you can guide your children in handling theirs.* You will need to let your children know what is an appropriate way to express emotions and what isn't, what they can and cannot say, and what they can and cannot do.

"You can be mad, but you can't hit your brother."

"You can be upset at your sister, but you can't call her names."

Obviously, any responses that hurt others or damage property won't be tolerated. In helping your children come up with a good solution, though, use questions:

"What do you think you could do?"

"What do you think might work?"

"What have you tried before? Let's list the things that we've never tried before. Then you can choose one and see if it helps."

"If you were in my place, what do you think I would suggest?"

As you develop your feelings vocabulary, the next step is to learn to *answer emotion with emotion.* Here are some examples of what this looks and sounds like:

"I can see that you're hurting [or sad or scared or feeling guilty or…]."

"It saddens me that you feel so alone at school."

"I can see how disappointed you are that you weren't invited to the party. I know that's disappointing to you."

"I can appreciate that you're upset about missing the game. I know that's disappointing to you."

"I know you're really frustrated right now because you're having trouble understanding algebra. I want you to know that I care about you and will help you in any way I can."

"I'm committed to going through this with you."

"Can you share with me how I've hurt you? How did it make you feel? I want to understand and make it right."

Some parents have done the following. They have taken the drawing of Elmer, the Emotions Elephant (see page 39), and made it much larger.

Whenever your child is struggling with some issue, you could say, "Let's go and find Elmer and have him help us discover what's going on inside right now." As you share this with your child, read off the various words (if your child is not able to read yet). Perhaps you could make a face to show what this emotion might look like. If your child reads, have him pick the word. You could ask him questions such as:

What's another word for this emotion?

What does _____ look like on your face?

What does _____ taste like?

What could we do with _____?

In time, you'll find that your child will be able to tell you what he's feeling. By doing this, especially with boys, you will help your son have a much better emotional balance in his life.

———◆———

Now, as we close this chapter, let's do some graphs. So you can begin to understand the impact of losses in your own life, I'd like you to complete a Loss History Graph for yourself. (See page 42.) Draw a line across a page. On the left put a zero, and on the right jot down your age today.

The next step is to sit back and come up with your earliest recollection.

Sometimes this is called the "dawn of memory." For most people, their first recollection takes them back to ages two to five. The memory could be good, bad, happy, sad, or neutral. It's just an event or experience. (I've talked to some folks who can remember being one year old or younger. But if there's no memory before five, it may be worth exploring the reason for this. Many have experienced such a painful event or trauma before this time that they blocked it out.)

Below is an example of one adult's Loss History Graph. The grief therapists who created this experience have found that those over the age of fourteen have at least five losses to plot. The length of the vertical line refers to the intensity of the loss event. The further the line goes down, the greater the loss. The shaded bar indicates that this loss is still affecting the person's life in some way.

After you complete your graph, ask yourself:

- What am I feeling about each loss?
- What does this tell me about the loss?
- Have I grieved over these losses or not?
- What work do I need to complete?

Susan's Graph

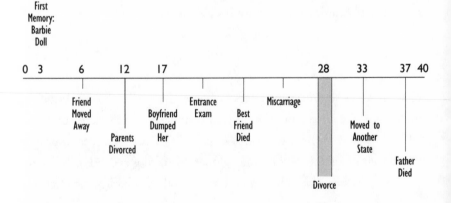

Now draw a graph for each of your children. Follow the same instructions, and complete the losses based on the losses you were aware of. Then spend time with your children and ask them to complete their own graphs if they're old enough. The following is Janice's loss chart for her ten-year-old daughter, Jean. The next is Jean's own chart. Do you see the differences? Do you see what Janice wasn't aware of? Perhaps your own child's loss graph will cause you to remember and identify losses from your own childhood—perhaps some things you were never aware of prior to this exercise.

Janice's Graph for Ten-Year-Old Jean

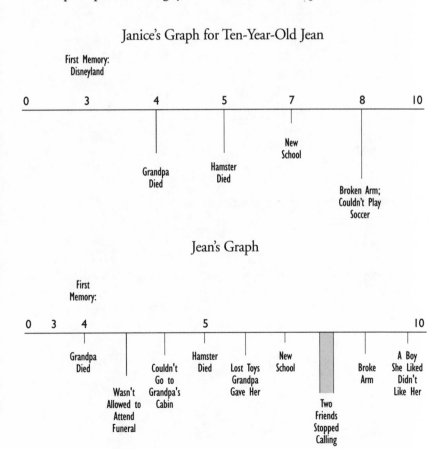

Jean's Graph

Your Loss History Graph

First Memory:

0 _____

Your Child's Loss History Graph

First Memory:

0 _____

Chapter 3

Don't Overlook These Two!

Dear Room and Tree House,

I'm sad because I spent my whole life with you. I have a lot of good memories. In my room you were dark at night so I could sleep. I liked the big window you had so I could go out and jump into the tree house (we won't tell Dad; he doesn't know). Good-bye to both of you. I will miss you. I hope another kid comes to live here so you won't be lonely for me.

Good-bye,

Fred

A short and sweet good-bye letter from nine-year-old Fred. He seems to be accepting his family's move...as he moves through all the sadness of letting go.

I wish all kids could do it like that. But some, as they face the shock, unmet expectations, and family silence accompanying the pain of loss, never verbalize their feelings as Fred did.

And they may never be invited to do it, because some losses simply get overlooked. Or their impact is severely underestimated. I'm talking about two of the most common losses of childhood: moving and losing a pet. Sometimes we fail to notice just how powerful these two events can be for our children. They blow into our families like gale-force storms, potentially wreaking havoc in our relationships. And since they can have such powerful impact, we do well to batten down the hatches and prepare for them while they're still on the far horizon.

Moving: Missing the Old, Familiar Places

How often have you moved from one residence to another as an adult? What was the experience like for you (aside from all the physical labor)? You were probably exhausted, not just from the work, but from orchestrating the lives of the children at such a chaotic time. You needed to keep tabs on *people* while transferring all the *things* from one house to another. You had plenty to keep you busy and very little time to consider what this move meant to you emotionally.

Did any of the children get lost in the shuffle?

A move affects everyone emotionally, especially children. I've known families to postpone a move until their children were at a transition stage, between elementary and middle school or between middle school and high school, so it would be easier. Those families seemed to know that when a child moves from one residence to another, it's a major loss experience.

It doesn't matter whether the new house or yard is larger or nicer or in a better neighborhood or if the move was near or far. It's still a move; it's still leaving the familiar. The children have grown accustomed to their old home, with its special places and smells and sounds. And losing that special place entails the loss of so much that comes packaged with it: friends, church, scouting group, sports activities, teachers, favorite stores, a backyard tree.

It's easy for parents to make mistakes at this time, since they're feeling the pressure and perhaps staggering under the load of all that must be done. Often the last thing they want to hear from their children is...

"But I really like it here."

"Why do we have to move?"

"Leave me here, Mom, and I can live at John's house."

"I don't want to leave all my friends."

"My team needs me!"

"Everybody's going to stare at the 'new kid.' I hate that!"

With the arrival of the moving van, a child is leaving his world as he knows it. And in the fiery heat of change, certain parental mistakes are sure to bubble to the surface. Here are a few to avoid.

1. Focusing only on the new. But what about the old—the old place, the old school, the old friends? Are children supposed to immediately erase their memory? Are they supposed to be just as excited as you are about the new job challenge, the lovely french doors, or the incredibly low mortgage rate?

No. Those are adult concerns.

Too often parents focus on the new life awaiting their children—

much of which is wonderful—and don't help them grieve the loss of their old life. The children hear:

"Don't feel so bad. C'mon, you know you'll make new friends."

"You'll have a much bigger room, you know."

"But it's such a short walk to school!"

"They have a great YMCA program in our new town."

"I saw a bunch of kids your age on the block."

The worst, of course, is the classic "Don't make Mommy and Daddy feel bad about this" pleading, which can be communicated in myriad ways, verbally or nonverbally.

But the child might legitimately answer, "Why not?" All your child's feelings are normal. If he doesn't grieve the loss of the familiar (perhaps making you feel a little bad), it's harder for him to connect with the new, the unfamiliar.

There are several practical steps you can take to honor the old—and even keep it somewhat accessible for a while. Help your child obtain phone numbers, street addresses, and e-mail addresses of the old friends. With e-mail it's so much easier to stay in touch. Of course, you'll want to be careful what you promise about future visits—either bringing your child back or having friends come and stay for a while. Be tentative about it, but, if possible, try to work this out together.

And don't forget to ask your child who or what she would like to say good-bye to when she leaves the old place. This can include not just *people*—such as friends, teachers, pastors, coaches, store clerks—but *places,* such as a park, an old hideout in the backyard, or a cherished bedroom.

2. Failing to do some physical prep work. A mom and dad told me their first move took place when one child was four and the other two. The two-year-old remembers his parents saying they were moving, and it wasn't a major move for him. But the oldest boy didn't remember being told and didn't realize the new house they arrived at would now be his new home! He recalls being in shock. He expected to return to his old house, but suddenly it was time to go to bed in a brand-new room.

Could physical preparation help? It did the next time around. Here's what I mean: This same family experienced the next move when their three boys were fourteen, twelve, and six. They moved into a newly constructed house in the same city. As a family, they had selected the lot, talked about the floor plan, watched the concrete flow into the foundation forms, observed carpenters hammering, sawing, and thrusting up the new walls. The kids were wide eyed and thrilled to be a part of each step. Every week they were there, watching things progress. What anticipation! There was little sense of loss in this situation.

Another aspect of prep work could apply to saying good-bye at preschool or school, a major transition for kids. If possible, make arrangements for your child to visit the new school and church and meet the significant people before you leave the old places. You might even ask to have your child paired with a new classmate and allowed to attend the school for a sample day. Imagine how helpful it would be if your child could walk around the school, days or weeks in advance, to discover the location of rooms, bathrooms, and the gym. If the move occurs during summertime, give some thought as to how your child can connect with future classmates prior to the opening bell.

3. Avoiding the emotional prep work. Whenever there's a move, you not only need to plan for it physically but emotionally as well. This takes time in the beginning but actually saves time and pain later on. You know the move is going to be an adjustment for the children (and you as well), so let everyone talk about their thoughts and feelings regarding it.

When your children talk, you will hear statements, ideas, and suggestions you probably don't want to hear. Just listen. Don't try to fix the problems or change their minds. If the children are younger, give them some crayons and have them draw their feelings about the move. Share your own mixture of excitement and sadness. If you have to move because of a family breakup, downscaling and economic loss, or armed-service deployment, you probably have some anger and bitterness to share as well.

For years I've suggested that, as a family, you go from room to room in the house, talk about your favorite memories in each room, and say good-bye to each room. The conjured memories can be profound and significant…or quite humorous. I think of seven-year-old Tim as he stood in the old bathroom with the family and said, "I remember when I was first able to stand and pee in this toilet." Heidi shared, "I'll miss hearing the branches from the tree scraping on the windows. Good-bye, tree. I'll miss you." Invite everyone to wave good-bye to each room or place.

You could even encourage your children to write a letter to your house or backyard, thanking it for all the good times and saying good-bye to each place. Children could leave a letter in each room or read the letter to each room.

4. Overlooking the impact of differing cultures. Four years later this same family moved from the thriving metropolis of Denver to a tiny town in Arkansas. For six months the five had to live in a small condo while their new home was being built. What a different culture they encountered in the small Southern city—the focus on agriculture, rodeo, and guns; the different way of talking; the miniature school-class sizes; the folksy, unhurried conversations; the unusual weather patterns; and—as all the girls quickly pointed out—the bugs! This move just wasn't so pleasant, and there were multiple intangible losses.

It was hard for the parents and the two oldest boys to watch the difficult adjustment of the ten-year-old. He'd left a core of six very close friends at a Christian school, where everybody seemed just like him. Now he had to ride a bus to school with students through high-school age. The way they talked and acted made him think he'd been abducted by aliens. He knew no one, and it took about six months to start connecting.

5. Minimizing the apparently "smaller" loss. If the move results from a family breakup due to divorce or death, an abundance of losses will follow. In the midst of these, it would be easy to overlook the loss of the move. (We'll talk about pets later, but here remember that sometimes a pet is a major loss when the family divorces. A child used to play with his pet every day, and now he only sees it every other weekend. And the child had nothing to say about what happened at this time.[1] My point is simply this: It's no good just focusing on the "big" losses while letting the seemingly smaller ones take their course. As we learned in the previous chapter, all losses are experienced at 100 percent; there is no "half grief."

6. Never really talking it through. Share your own feelings to let your children know it's all right to talk about this move. Some of the kids might be very angry toward you (or those responsible for "making" them move). How will you begin? Some parents start like this:

"I'm looking forward to this move, because _____. But I'm also sad since I will be leaving _____."

"I'm not looking forward to this move, because _____. But we have to do it. Let's talk about why we don't like moving."

After making a statement like one of these, discuss what you could all look forward to and how you could work together to make the move better.

Or suppose the kids' grandparents told of some of their experiences in moving when they were children. The purpose of such stories would be to help your children tell their own stories and, especially, share their feelings.

If you have several children, expect differences in their responses to the move. Some will show their concern outwardly, while others will "stuff" their emotions and appear unaffected. But it's a loss for everyone. Some children are more stressed and upset about ending a chapter in their lives or about facing the *loss* of the known and the *fear* of the unknown. Encouraging the children to share their feelings, validating their concerns, helping them say good-bye—all of this will help the entire family say hello to the new location.

However, you may need to educate your children's school and church about the importance of saying good-bye. Some schools have a good-bye ceremony or party. Some assemble a scrapbook of letters and drawings as a good-bye gift, or they have all the classmates sign a card or T-shirt. The same could be done at church. The pastor could ask the family to come forward for a good-bye and a prayer of dedication. They could stand with the pastor following the service to let the entire church family say its good-byes.

PETS: WHEN ROVER GOES AWAY

"It's just a pet. Don't be so upset."

"You knew it had to die someday, so you should have been ready for this."

"Hey, real people have died in this family. So what's the big deal about Fluffy?"

Sadly, such statements abound in our families. And the words sear the hearts of children who have lost a pet they truly loved. Even viewing a floating goldfish (remember?) can be upsetting—even if Grandpa died just last month. The pet still counts; its death still hurts.

See it from the children's point of view. The pet has become a loyal companion and confidant. Interaction with this animal friend has taught the children many of life's lessons, such as loyalty, trust, love, compassion, and empathy. But that pet will likely also be one of the first losses for children, especially since a pet typically lives one-fifth as long as a person. And for some children, as they grow into adulthood, such a loss will be repetitive.

Children often bond to their pets more than their parents bond to those animals. They form deep, emotional attachments to their dog or cat or hamster or guinea pig. They provide the pet with the best of care, and some children and pets are inseparable. An only child may even view the pet as a sibling. A sick child may see the pet as a source of comfort and protection. After all, a pet will play with a child when others won't. Children, in particular, are at risk for a significant amount of grief with a pet loss—whether it comes by dying, getting lost, or moving with the other household in a divorce.

What have children said about pets?

"He's my best friend."

"I can tell him anything."

"He listens to me when my daddy won't."

"I feel safe at night 'cause he's in my room."

"He likes to see me come home from school. He always waits at the window."

So if a pet dies, keep in mind this could be the first personal friend of your child to die. And it will also be one of his or her first learning experiences about illness and death. That's the potentially positive note: The grief your child experiences over this loss teaches that death is part of the process of life. All of us will need to learn that sooner or later.

How can you help when Rover is no more? Let me suggest a few basic dos and don'ts.

DO face your own grief. This could be a double burden for you if you were especially close to this pet. Yet your own grief needs to be confronted squarely and with all the emotion it carries. Your child will see your sadness. Tell her that it's the pet's death that makes you sad, not anything the pet did.

DON'T "fudge" the truth. You've probably heard this story: A little girl's cat died. Her mom told her it had gone to heaven. The girl pondered this for a moment and then asked, "Why would God want a dead cat?"

The point is, when you tell your child about the death of the animal (or impending death), be completely aboveboard with the facts. If the pet was euthanized, say so—not that it was "put down," put to sleep, or ran away. Often euthanasia is a family decision, and it's discussed fully. Then each person can decide whether he or she wants to attend or not. Tell your child what to expect in the room, in a way he will understand. If your child doesn't want to be in the room, give him the opportunity to see the animal after it has died.

DO make room for questions—all of them. Young children will ask and ask and ask. Keep making time and energy for those questions. If you must euthanize your pet, be ready for "Why does he have to die? I don't want him to die!"

Explain why it's necessary. "Old Buster has been suffering, honey, because his body has worn out and isn't working well anymore." Or, "Blacky had a disease that medicine or treatment couldn't fix anymore." Or, "Mops had an accident when she ran into the street. The car ran over him, and it was so bad he couldn't be fixed. Nothing will help him."

Always ask your children if they have any questions about the way their pet died or about anything related to the event. Be prepared to be stumped. If you don't know an answer, say so. Don't give quick answers to make your children feel better, such as, "Of course Mops will be in heaven with us."

DON'T neglect good-byes in word and deed. This is a time for the entire family to talk about their companion who died. Sometimes the family members select their favorite photo of their pet to have on display for a month. Or they draw a picture of the pet or just talk about how they felt when they saw the pet for the first time. If you have videos, watch them together. Share about your favorite experiences with the pet.

Describe your pet's personality. Who did he most look like and act like in your family? What do you miss the most about your pet? Also share verbally or in a drawing the feelings you have about your pet's death.

Our first golden retriever died at the age of twelve, five months before this was written. He had thyroid cancer, and his body simply wore out. We had many memories. We acquired Sheffield eight months after our son Matthew died, so we were still deep in our grief. Therefore, we established a special connection with this beautiful animal.

Sheffield learned to bring in the newspaper and answer the portable phone. He even served as a therapy dog in counseling. His puppyhood days created many memories for us, including chewing up my wife's glasses, eating a Christmas-tree light bulb, chewing the garden hose into four pieces, and getting river rocks stuck in his stomach (requiring emergency surgery). But such things are all part of the joy and challenge of raising a puppy. He inspired the creation of two books about dogs: *A Friend Like No Other* and *Everything I Know About Parenting, I Learned from My Puppy.*

Some children will want to see the body, and some won't. Saying good-bye to your pet like this can help the grieving process, but it shouldn't be forced, especially if the body of the animal has been severely traumatized—mangled in an accident, for example, or half-eaten by another animal. In any case, children do need some kind of memorial service. Show pictures, if necessary, and invite each person to say good-bye. Afterward, some pets are buried in the backyard, some left at the vet, and some cremated.

DO remember to keep checking in. Periodically, over the weeks and months, ask your children what they're thinking or feeling about the pet who died. You could begin with, "You know, I was thinking about Puff today and how she used to sit in the window and look out. What do you remember about her?" You could use stories or pictures with younger children if their vocabularies are limited. Below is a pet discussion guide that you could use with your children.

DON'T forget to enlist others. Loving support is available for your child and family when a beloved pet dies. So let neighbors, friends, teachers, and relatives know what has occurred, and enlist their caring and

Let's Remember Our Pet

To the parent: Use this outline as a simple discussion guide when talking with your child about a pet that has died. Use your own words, and keep the conversation as natural as possible. Remember, these questions are only suggestions to help you get started. Your child may take the conversation along different paths. Be ready to follow where he or she leads.

Let's talk about _____. I wonder what her name meant to you.

I wonder what you said to _____ that you could share with me.

Did you celebrate _____'s birthday? How?

What do you wish you could have said to _____ before she died?

Did she ever talk to you? If so, what did she say?

Was _____ a member of our family? How could you tell?

I wonder which of these happened to you. Did _____

    …love you? How do you know?

    …make you feel needed and important? Talk about it.

    …comfort you when you were sad? If so, how?

    …ever get angry with you? What happened?

    …help you be more responsible? If so, how?

How could you say good-bye to _____?

practical help. Let them know how your child might be feeling or behaving at the time, and indicate what they can expect. If some of the folks aren't familiar with how a person who is your child's age thinks and talks, forewarn them. Your child's graphic bluntness may throw them. Some of these people may not be pet lovers, and you may need to tell them that, on a scale of one to ten, this loss for your child was a ten.

When it comes to loss of a pet—or all the losses that come with moving—the key is to remember that *each child will grieve in a different way and for a different amount of time.* If the intense sadness or anger goes on for more than five or six months, however, you may want to seek professional help.

As for immediately replacing Rover? No. Don't obtain a new pet right away, even if your child pressures you for one. The grieving process needs time.

Chapter 4

Sickness...and All Its Big Questions

The young mother sat before me with tension carved into her brow. Her words and gestures spoke of weariness as she unveiled the tragic story of little Sarah.

Norm, it's just so tough letting the doctors put poison into your little girl's body....

And it all happened so fast. We'd gone to church that Sunday, and afterward Scott and I went to pick up our two-year-old from the nursery. One of the ladies told us she thought Sarah's stomach looked "funny"—and she felt a spot on Sarah's abdomen that seemed hard. She wondered whether we should take Sarah to see a doctor....

You know how mothers can sense things? We headed to the local children's hospital, and I knew something serious was going on as soon as the pediatric surgeon scheduled a CAT scan. Afterward he looked grim, telling us it was something called a

Wilms' tumor, a kidney cancer, but that it was still encapsulated. Sarah went into the hospital and had surgery the next evening.

Did I say things happened fast? I couldn't believe what was happening. I felt like I was just along for the ride—on a speeding, out-of-control freight train headed for a cliff! But the surgeon was positive, and Sarah came through surgery without a hitch. Then, the day after, it's like the horrible reality hit us hard. Reading about kidney tumors pulled us down—we're talking about a cancer that would require chemotherapy for the next eighteen weeks!

Chemo. Poison!

I hate it, but she had to have it.

When we first started, I thought I was ready for my beautiful little blonde to lose her curls. But after four weeks—and thinking that maybe the hair wouldn't go after all—we were cuddling on the couch, and those golden, silky strands started coming out in handfuls.

My heart was breaking, Norm, looking at all that hair covering my fingers. Within a few days it all fell out.

And I wasn't prepared for all the comments, either! Even if she was wearing pink ribbons and flowers, people still thought Sarah was a boy. Sometimes I'd let them know she was in the middle of chemotherapy and had lost her hair; other times it just seemed like too much work to say anything at all.

It was scary thinking, "What's next?" because of all the possible side effects. Like, for instance, the chemo got to Sarah's muscles, and her right eye began to droop. And two of her medicines made her really sick. I mean, it's so heartbreaking when your two-year-old knows to run to the bathroom and throw up in the toilet.

Her immune system got real weak during these treatments. The two of us, Scott and I, became homebodies. Even going to the grocery store seemed dangerous. If Sarah were to run a fever, she'd have to get to the hospital quickly. I did everything I could to keep that from happening.

Her brothers lost out on a lot. Our ten-year-old missed his baseball team's pizza party on the day Sarah went into the hospital, and everything seemed to snowball from there. Friends couldn't come over, things we'd always done as a family were put on hold, and we became almost like hermits in our own home.

Then the kids' grades began to suffer, and their personality quirks kept getting worse. My youngest son is a dreamer, and his teacher told me that he just "wasn't there" during class. My oldest son stopped caring about his grades altogether. When he didn't understand his math, instead of getting help from us or the teacher, he decided to fail the section. When we yelled, he didn't even care. It took another section—and the threat of summer school—to get him back on track.

We were planning to go to Wisconsin for a family vacation this summer, but because of Sarah, it's not going to work out. We're all bummed. And the oncologist has said it'll be a good six months before her immune system is up and running again.

So what can I say? We never expected anything like this! It's so hard.

Yet there's blessing, too. I mean, people have been so supportive at church. And it feels like God is right there, helping us keep a positive attitude...most of the time. Looking back, we realize things could have gone far differently. But like any other parent, I would never wish something like this on my child. Or my family.

I've let Sarah's story unfold at length so you could feel some of the heartache that serious illness brings into a family. Or maybe you've already been there—or you are in the midst of a health crisis right now in your own family. If not, you may well face such a situation in the future.

In any case, I believe such traumatic circumstances raise critical questions in every parent's thinking. Will you allow me to try to anticipate and answer some of those questions? With that in mind, I've organized this chapter around Three Big Questions I often hear when a family's major loss is all about being sick.

BIG QUESTION #1: WHAT ARE THE SPECIAL CHALLENGES OF CHRONIC ILLNESS?

This may not be an easy section for you to read. None of us wants our children to be sick with any disorder, let alone a chronic illness. But it may happen. And here's what's so important to know: As the parent, you will be the key person assisting your child through the loss process.

It will be you, not the doctor.

One mother finally realized how much of a challenge and a calling her child's illness would be to her. At age five her boy was diagnosed with spinal muscular atrophy, a form of muscular dystrophy. She puts it like this:

> I got mail from the Muscular Dystrophy Society and threw it away for a whole year. I was a basket case. Although my family couldn't have been more supportive, I kept thinking, *You don't know what I am going through.* In our very large families, no one had ever had anything like this happen. It was a fluke that my husband and I both had these genes.
>
> Finally I went to a parents' meeting. I met a mother who spent 13

years being a mess, taking drugs, and feeling very sorry for herself. That did it for me. *I'm not going to be like that. That's not what I want for my child. I am going to be positive, to give him the best I can.* I began to realize with this disease you can't really forget. I am learning that I have to constantly adapt to different changes in his body. As I became more honest with myself, I was more honest with him. The disease just progresses, and I have to make a new adjustment, and so does he. But we are living, and that is what is important.[1]

Moms and dads will struggle between their own fear and shock and being supportive (as well as an advocate) for their sick children.

Of course, we expect children to be under the weather once in a while. Children get sick; it's what they do. They get colds, flu, chickenpox, viruses, and hives. Dozens of times as they're growing up, you'll tell your child:

"You have a cold."

"Oh, it's the flu."

"Look at those red dots. I think you have measles."

"It looks like it's your asthma again."

"I think you may have eaten the wrong thing. That's why you're throwing up."

But what if sickness moves to the next level—meningitis, strep throat, chronic ear infections, asthma, pneumonia? All of these can disrupt a family's plans and functioning. Yet these maladies, usually thought of as *acute* illnesses, are still to be expected.

On the other hand, *chronic* illnesses—conditions with a long duration or recurring quality—are strictly for the kid down the block, right? It's not supposed to happen to us! When I had a light case of polio at age nine, I remember my mom consulting ten doctors until we had a diagnosis. Such circumstances can change family routines as life centers around hospital visits or the giving of meds or extensive trips to the specialist. Family rituals and traditions may undergo a tremendous change, and "normal" life can become a thing of the past (imagine celebrating Thanksgiving on the "wrong" day—or in the hospital).

If a child has a chronic illness, it can mean lots of school absences, isolation from friends, limited sports activity. The most common chronic illnesses are asthma, severe allergies, arthritis, diabetes, seizure disorders, and cancer. Such illnesses can cause mental and physical disability. And, of course, a myriad of possible accidents can change the child's and family's life dramatically.

Talk about special challenges!

But let's delve a little deeper into the primary challenge hitting us right at the beginning: a diagnosis. As a parent, you will be in shock when you hear the diagnosis of a serious disease or disorder. Your head will spin with a sense of disbelief, of unreality. *This happens to other children, not us.* And your first response may be to distance yourself from the news: *It must be wrong. The doctor's mistaken. It's someone else's child.* The diagnosis itself is a major loss for you as well as your child.

Then comes the pain of hearing about the treatment, and finally you listen to the doctor's prediction about your future: the prognosis. Some diagnoses are quick and easy, others longer and more difficult, involving numerous specialists. Treatment can vary from noninvasive and simple to invasive and high-tech. Prognosis, too, will vary from quite positive to maddeningly tentative.

The more complex any of these three elements are, the more of a roller-coaster ride you're in for as the parent. These three don't always follow a sequential order either. A tentative diagnosis requires a treatment before you may have a full diagnosis and prognosis. This could result in additional treatment, which can affect the prognosis. So it's rarely a simple process. It's a challenge from the beginning.

BIG QUESTION #2: WHAT'S GOING TO HAPPEN WHEN A SERIOUS ILLNESS HITS MY CHILD?

There's no easy way to say this: Now much of your life will revolve around your child's illness and its effects. There will be special meals, cancelled vacations, a change in living conditions, trips to the doctor or hospital or pharmacy, searches for as much information and help as you can find. Your child with the illness experiences losses, you experience losses, and so do the other children in the household. Their needs don't change, but your time, attention, and energy do. A child's illness can impact your marriage and your job as well.

Actually, you're called on to transform your role. You were the parent of a healthy child. Now you're thrust into the role of a parent of a seriously ill, chronically ill, or disabled child.[2] The shock of it can keep you from hearing and absorbing what the doctors are saying to you. You may have to hear the diagnosis and prognosis again and again. And you will grieve over many factors, even if the illness is curable with treatment.

I've met with many parents who were raising disabled children with one condition or another. To them, a life revolving around this child was often the only kind of life they knew. They had never experienced another lifestyle. But for you there is shock and radical change. This level of self-sacrifice is brand-new...and comes brimming with fears.

You will need to face your emerging fears at this time. You will probably be afraid that your child will suffer horribly, afraid he or she won't recover, afraid that you can't handle all the responsibility, and afraid your child may die (even when nothing has been said about this). If your child is terminal, you'll likely fear that you won't be able to handle the grief.[3]

And what about all the questions from friends, grandparents, and church members about your child's condition? You'll need to answer, even though you may not have digested all the information. In fact, you may need to hear all the information again, take notes, and then write everything out. Some parents send a detailed letter to everyone who is concerned so they can avoid having to explain the situation multiple times each day.

You will receive unsolicited advice and guidance from others who feel they know best. Some may even insist that you follow what they say. This could leave you wondering whether you really are doing all you could be doing.

When I was counseling on the staff of a large church, I met a mother whose nine-year-old daughter was born with some of her organs on the outside of her body. The girl lacked a bladder, and the mom's life revolved around visiting doctors and clinics, looking for specialists, and raising the funds needed for the creation of a new bladder. In addition, this mom had to find the right childcare personnel and the right school, where her daughter's diapers could be changed every hour to keep her from developing a rash. She did all this while running her household—and holding down a job as an engineer!

So...what's going to happen when serious illness hits your family?

Life as you know it will be over. You'll take up a new life—a scary, busy, new life filled with incredible challenges. It may well be filled with awesome blessings, too, as so many parents of faith and courage have testified.

BIG QUESTION #3: WHAT'S IT ACTUALLY LIKE FOR MY SUFFERING CHILD?

When children are sick, their fear grows.

"When do I get better?"

"What's going to happen to me today?"

"Is this going to really hurt?"

"Who is this new person?"

"What are they going to do now?"

One five-year-old boy was very open about his condition and would tell everyone, "I have spinal muscular atrophy, and it makes my muscles weak, and if I can't walk right or if I fall, it's not my fault. If you have any questions, just ask me." He had a friend with the same condition who wouldn't talk about the problem nor let anyone help him.

Children do vary in their acceptance of their illness. Let's look at three of the younger ages separately.

Infants. The youngest children will be significantly affected by your stress and anxiety. So remember that it's very easy to transfer your emotions to children. How will you know? They may become unresponsive. Or, lacking verbal ability, they may express discomfort through irritability or fretfulness. Along with these possible responses, your children may become overly attached to you—clinging and not wanting the care of others.

Toddlers. Toddlers can be frustrated by illness; it limits their main goal in life: exploration. Constant doctor and therapy visits can produce angry responses. Children at this age level will sense your moods as well. Toddlers have limited language skills with which to express themselves, but they can understand many of your words. So you need to be careful what you say around them to friends, family, the doctor, nurse, and anyone over the phone. At this age, illness can lead to tantrums and throwing toys. The toddler has lost his freedom and ability to explore when he's sick.

Preschoolers. If preschool children have to be hospitalized, their main concern is being separated from their parents. In children three to four years old, new fears surface, including the fear of mutilation. That is, by now they may have seen death firsthand. They may have seen a car run over a small animal or may have watched a cat tear apart a bird. And so they might associate getting sick or dying with their bodies being mutilated. What if they've watched episodes of *ER* or *CSI* or the surgery channel? If blood has to be taken by a nurse, they're fixated by the sight of that vial being filled with crimson liquid.

Young children who repeatedly have to go in for testing are often bribed by their parents so they won't get upset.[4] But there are better ways. For example, some parents provide their children with a play doctor's kit and encourage them to act out what they're experiencing. This may be an opportunity to discover what their feelings are at this time.

Can illness or disability be explained to the preschool age group? Yes, since they can begin to understand *the process.* Sometimes pictures, picture books, or stories can convey a limited message. Or you may need to create your own visual aids.

When you go to urgent care, the doctor, the hospital, or a therapist, have the practitioner explain, in your child's vocabulary, what is occurring. You may not fully know how much your child can understand, but make the attempt to convey everything clearly and with emotional equilibrium.

Also, when illness hits your preschooler, be prepared for one question after another. When she asks questions, she wants answers. You may not have all the answers. Be sure to let her know that you will try to find some answers.

Preschoolers are quite aware of their bodies, so anything that affects their bodies will be the focus of their attention. This is where magical thinking comes into play along with a skewed sense of cause and effect. As one child said, "I didn't take my nap the other day; that's why I got sick. Today if I take my nap, my sick will go away." Another child stated, "I told my tummy to hurt so I could stay home. I shouldn't tell it that, 'cause now it hurts. I don't want to hurt like this. I have to tell it to stop hurting, and it will." At this age, kids believe their words and actions have so much power!

At the most basic level, your child is looking to you to take away the "ouch." But you may not be able to do that. You can be there to give comfort though. And you can help create a sense of normalcy amid the pain by working together on the daily tasks and decisions this illness calls forth. For instance, a preschooler can respond to the following:

"What clothes would you like to wear to the doctor today? What do you want him to see?"

"What color bandage would you like to wear today?"

"Which doll would you like to tell a story to about the brace on your leg?"

"Would you like to help me make a pill chart? Then you can keep track of which ones you take each day."

Kids at any age. What practical things can you do to help your child cope, no matter how old he or she is? The most important thing I can say is this: *You know your child better than anyone else.*

Remember that! Then do what you think is best. Listen to your own intuition more than the cacophony of voices around you offering so-called wisdom.

Especially if you have a concern for the doctor to know about, be sure to mention it. For years my wife and I faced the medication needs of our retarded child. We went through several different varieties, including phenobarbital and Dilantin. Matthew's doctor told my wife that she would know better than anyone else what Matthew's needs were, since she was closest to him day by day. On a number of occasions, my wife would come to me and say she was changing the meds because of such and such event or a report from Matthew. And the doctors would confirm her decisions.

A Few More Nagging Questions— and Some Quick Answers

I've heard lots of questions from parents when chronic illness hits. In fact, the questions swirl endlessly and seem to multiply as the tragedy deepens. They are too numerous to cover in one book like this; however, here are some of the most common ones, along with my brief responses—

How do I break the bad news? This is a tough one! Your child feels sick and knows something is quite wrong. But he's not aware of what it is. If you find yourself in this situation, don't try to sugarcoat the problem or be evasive. Simply state the facts to him. For example:

"You have a condition called asthma. It means that you'll have to carry some medicine around with you."

"You have a disease called AIDS. You will need treatment for this."

"You have a ruptured disk in your back. We will show you the pictures of it so you can see what we're talking about. In time the doctor will perform surgery to help correct the problem."

"You have cancer. You'll be receiving treatment for this over a period of weeks."

You don't need to go into extensive detail, but be ready for questions, which are likely to be repeated. Don't let the repetition annoy you. Calmly answer each time. Children need to get used to the new state of reality.

And, yes, use the medical terms so your child becomes accustomed to his condition. But remember that your child is still a person and should be talked about as a person, not as a disease or a condition. Too often in medical environments caretakers can slip into the habit of referring to a person like this:

"He's the CP boy."

"The epileptic girl."

"The cancer kid."

"The broken neck in room 125."

No. He is a child with cerebral palsy or epilepsy or cancer or serious injury. He's still a kid coping with life's challenges, as must we all.

At what age can my child begin to understand what's really happening? Do very young children understand grief and its process? Yes, and this is a time to talk with them about the process.[5]

At virtually any age you can assist your child in learning as much as possible about the disease or disability. Books, the Internet, and interviews can give your child a feeling of some control. As with other losses, providing some way of saying good-bye to what was lost or missed will be helpful at this time.

A new level of understanding occurs with young elementary-age children. These children can separate fantasy from reality. And they will understand the duration and characteristics of a cold or the flu as well as serious illness. A serious illness makes them different from their schoolmates. And whether another child or adult ever says it, they begin to feel their illness is a part of their identity. One six-year-old said, "I'm slow because of my disease. Other kids tease me; sometimes I wish they wouldn't. I don't like it. I have told them what I have. But they don't understand. The other day we had a contest in one of my subjects. I knew all the answers. The other children were surprised. Now they want to play with me."

What if people stare—or other kids make fun? If you're out somewhere, and someone is staring at your child, and your child is aware of it, you have several options. You could just explain to your child that this person doesn't know what to say or is wondering about his condition. That's natural.

Another possibility is to go to that person with your child and say, "I noticed your concern about Timmy. Would you like to hear our story?"

Sadly, I've also heard people talk about the child, in his presence, as if he weren't there or was some kind of nonperson. If possible, you could ask the person who is staring, "Why don't you ask Jimmy about his condition? He's quite capable of telling you what's going on in his life."

But what about the kids looking on—the ones who can be pretty cruel with their remarks at times? I've heard numerous insensitive comments, even from adults, including:

"What's wrong with her?"

"How do you go to the bathroom?"

"You should have noticed her symptoms earlier."

"Is this a genetic problem in your family?"

"If you knew this, why did you have children?"

"Does somebody have to feed you?"

"Gross! Look at her _____."

"Shouldn't you keep her at home, away from other children?"

These are difficult statements to deal with. Several parents have shared with me that they forewarned their children about what they could expect from others. They prepared them for how to respond. You could begin a discussion toward that end like this:

- "Sometimes other kids stare because what they see they've never seen before. What do you think *they're* thinking?"

- "Another child may come up and say, 'What's wrong with you?' What do you think you could say?"
- "Sometimes you won't be able to play the games the other children are playing. What could you do at that time?"
- "Some children might make fun of you or call you names. How do you think you will feel when that happens? What do you think you could say if that happens?"
- "Let's think together what you could say to your classmates if you get sick or there's a smell."

How are we going to handle school? Some disabilities don't limit learning, of course. But if weeks are missed, sometimes children can't catch up. They lose out on school activities, outings, friends' parties, etc. They begin to feel "out of the group." One seven-year-old said, "I'm always by myself. I don't have friends like I used to. I hate my sickness. I'm mad at Mommy for not finding a doctor to make me well."

The child's life changes when school is affected so much. I missed an entire semester in fourth grade because of polio. Fortunately, I had skipped a half grade prior to that, so I ended up at the right grade level eventually. But I felt as if I had missed six months of my life with friends.

The key is for you to get to know teachers and school administrators personally. Be ready with all the information these folks will need to make sure your child can function in the rough-and-tumble environment of a public-school setting. If this will be too difficult for your child—and only you can tell, based on your child's physical and mental condition—then seek out tutors and home teachers. Or invest in homeschooling curriculum, and get ready for your added role as World's Greatest Teacher.

Part II

Seeing the Whole-Family Dynamic

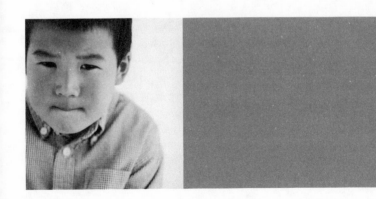

Chapter 5

In the Family "Machine"— Each Part Affected!

D r. Charlotte Thompson tells the story of a pediatrician who grew up with a disabled sibling. The family knew something was wrong with her brother, but the problem wasn't diagnosed until he was fifteen. He wasn't expected to do chores or have outside jobs like the other children. The parents had time and money for him, but they had very little of either for the other kids. They put up with temper tantrums and angry explosions from him but wouldn't tolerate any expression of anger from the others.

The disabled child knew his favored status. He used it to his advantage, being viewed as "the good child." The others were the bad ones.

You've been carrying your brother on your back all of your life, which is probably one of the reasons you went into pediatrics. You have been trying to understand what happened with your brother and why you always felt him around your neck like a millstone. You have a highly overdeveloped sense of responsibility toward other children and have tried to mother the world. This has caused emotional problems, marital problems, and has left you feeling drained, angry and incomplete.

Essentially you have had to be your own parent, and after your parents died, you felt a tremendous responsibility for your brother. By transferring his dependence from your parents to you, you created a very difficult problem for yourself. You may well know that people often grow to dislike, or even hate, the individuals on whom they feel dependent. This was surely your brother's case. First he hated your parents, and now he hates you.[1]

How complicated our losses and responses can become! Could that situation have been avoided if the parents had communicated with the other children and they had all worked together as a team? I believe it's possible. But who helps parents know how to respond to the *other* children when their sibling is chronically ill or deceased?

Thankfully, research is providing parents with helpful information about what to expect when there's a sick or disabled child in the family. Now we can prepare for the complex reactions that tend to reverberate through the family system.

We need to become experts at interpersonal responses and reactions. We might even view the family as a kind of flesh-and-blood machine with myriad working parts and processes. If one part goes off kilter—gets "damaged" or completely broken—can we predict how the rest of the machinery will act in response?

Yes! Let's stand back and observe that struggling machine to see what happens. How will it function now? What actions and reactions will become evident, spurred by the weakened or missing part? In the family, when a child is sick or dies, the reactions have to do with *how everybody else is affected and how they'll respond.*

How the Siblings Might Act and React

I'll begin this section by simply listing some of the basic tidbits of information that recent research has been able to gather. Let these facts and trends sink in as your basic orientation to the topic.

- Older siblings adjust better than younger children to having a brother or sister with disabilities—with the exception of the eldest daughter, who doesn't adjust as well.
- Eldest daughters are often given the task of caring for the child with special needs. They take up this role more often than any other children in the family.
- Children are more affected by having a sibling with a disability if that sibling is of the same gender.
- If there are only two children in the family and one has a disability, the other is more pressured to fulfill the parents' hopes and dreams for success in their children. If the nondisabled child is a girl, she is also assigned more care-giving responsibility.
- Siblings of children with disabilities tend to show positive qualities of being well adjusted, mature beyond their years, tolerant of differences in people, helpful toward people, and aware of social needs.
- Siblings can be excellent teachers of their brothers and sisters with disabilities because they are in a different position in the family. (That is, all the children aren't lumped together as "the kids," as is typical in most families.)
- Siblings may judge the worth of their friends by the friends' reactions to their brother or sister with the disability.
- Siblings may experience guilt as they surpass a disabled older brother or sister in skills and abilities.

- Siblings may feel pressure to overachieve.
- Siblings may overidentify with a mildly disabled brother or sister. Or as they reach teen years, they may not consider a severely disabled sibling a "person."
- Siblings may feel that requests by parents for help with the brother or sister are an intrusion on their time. Conversely, they may view such requests as a privileged opportunity to cooperate with the parents.[2]

Clearly, children are greatly affected when one of their siblings is sick or disabled. They have a greater-than-usual level of neediness. They want more nurturing from their parents at a time when their parents have less to give. When a loss or crisis arises, too often no one thinks about talking to the other children about what's going on and why. Consequently, they continue to struggle with their feelings, their questions, and their emotional pain. They may feel alone and quite angry.

After all, when a child is ill, it's easy for parents to pamper him. The more that happens, the more the siblings tend to be negative and less supportive. Sometimes sick children are actually treated like heroes. They receive gifts and special privileges, and sometimes celebrities are even asked to entertain them.

Sometimes, out of guilt and a sense of futility in not being able to do much else to help the child, parents resort to indulging the son or daughter. The sibling's response might be frustration and envy, evidenced by becoming whiney or developing psychosomatic ailments. This is the sibling's way to get some attention as well as some of those privileges. In fact, some siblings wish their sick brother or sister were dead so life could get back to the way it used to be.[3]

I'm speaking here of attention-getting mechanisms. If parents try to ignore these attempts to gain attention, siblings may intensify their efforts by using drugs, running away, setting fires, or destroying property. Expressed rage is certainly one way to get attention![4]

But suppose you don't see much of a change in your other children? This could happen. Many children hide their distress and have to deal with it years later in adulthood. Be alert to children who seem quiet and unaffected. Come alongside them and gently, as the time passes, keep providing opportunities for emotional expression.

Finally, remember that children raised with a disabled sibling often feel a strong sense of responsibility, either self-imposed or placed on them by their parents. Therefore you may see a very positive change as the child decides to be "the good daughter." It is her means of survival. She makes few demands on her exhausted and stressed parents, and she tries to be helpful. But she, too, has needs her parents must meet. She also requires an opportunity to grieve.

How Parents Might Respond to the Siblings

You may be aware that you're not doing what you want or need to do with the other children. Your grief drains your energy and depletes the emotional investment you want to make in them. So you feel you're not being the parent you want to be, which adds to your frustration and sense of failure. But during the onset of the loss or crisis with your child, remember this: It's unrealistic to think you can act the way you want with the other children. You just don't have enough to give.

You'll also fluctuate in your feelings and responses to your children. You may feel resentment that your other children are healthy or still living, don't seem to be as concerned or grieving enough, or have adjusted too soon. Part of your response is your anger over the unfairness of what has happened. You may feel you can't invest what you want or you've lost your ability to give. Or you may be afraid to invest because something bad could happen to these children. You could also overreact and overprotect. I raise all of these possible difficulties, because just being aware of them may help you to avoid them.[5]

It's interesting that choosing a helping profession as a vocation is common among the siblings of disabled people. Sometimes the other children carry guilt, feelings of responsibility, or a sense of chronic sorrow or sadness into adulthood. So they determine to devote their lives to "solving" the problem. Recall our unhappy pediatrician?

Sometimes the acceptance of a disabled brother or sister gets harder as kids grow older. As a daughter of some friends put it, "I grow older and change. But my sister stays the same, and at times it seems as though she goes backward. She's an adult like I am, but I'm a real adult, and she's still in infancy. And she always will be. That's sad."

Siblings face numerous pressures that we don't even think about. What does a child say to others when asked about a younger brother who just died? What does a child say to others when asked about a sibling who doesn't look disabled in any way but is nonverbal? Sometimes the less severe the impairment, the more difficult it is for the siblings, since they may feel embarrassed about their brother's or sister's behavior.

How Siblings Might React to the Sick Child

We wondered how Matthew, our retarded son, affected our daughter, Sheryl. (Matthew was born with his disability several years after Sheryl. When Matthew died at twenty-two, he was about eighteen months old mentally.) She seemed to handle his presence all right, but we weren't always sure.

One particular incident stands out. One day when Matthew was very young, Sheryl was at the house of a neighbor who had a baby three months younger than Matthew. That baby was turning over and sitting up. Sheryl came home and asked why their baby was able to do those things and Matthew wasn't, even though he was older. When Joyce told her that Matthew was "slower" and wouldn't be able to turn over for a while, Sheryl didn't say anything. But the hurt was visible on her face.

As Sheryl grew older, she never hid from the fact that her brother was mentally retarded. She never shielded the fact from her friends. We wondered whether she'd be embarrassed about it, but apparently she wasn't. She would bring her friends home, and when they met Matthew, she'd casually say, "This is my brother, Matthew. He's retarded." Then she would go on with what she was doing. Her friends were the ones who didn't seem to know how to respond. Yet as Sheryl moved through junior and senior high school, we noticed that she seemed to be sensitive to the needs of other retarded people and quite protective if others mistreated them.

When Sheryl was about thirty, I asked her how Matthew had affected her and what problems she had experienced in having a disabled brother. Here's her response:

> I can't think of any problems I had with Matthew being retarded when I was young. I didn't feel left out in any way. In fact, my first memory of Matthew was when Grandma and I were taking him for a stroll around the block, and he had a seizure. Grandma became very upset. I went to a house, knocked on the door, told the lady that my brother was having a seizure, and asked to borrow a spoon. The lady and I held him and used the spoon in his mouth so he wouldn't choke. I wasn't upset. It made me feel like I was really a part of the family since I could help him.
>
> His condition didn't really bother me. It was like riding in an

airplane or going through an earthquake when I was a child. I didn't fully understand the significance and all the ramifications of those situations nor of retardation.

But when I became an adult, I understood. Then it was difficult to deal with. I couldn't handle going to Matthew's home and seeing all the other disabled children. It just tore me to pieces. I have a difficult time seeing retarded children now.

After Sheryl said that, we talked a bit more. I told her I understood and have a similar response and sensitivity to seeing anyone with a disability. It took me years to discover what I was feeling was the wish that I could reach out and heal that person—make him or her whole—followed by the frustration of knowing I couldn't do it.

Sheryl floored me with her response: "I don't think Matthew's retardation was something for us to try to heal. I think his purpose was to bring healing to all of us. We're all different because of him. I know I'm a different person because of Matthew."

I just stood there silently, letting the truth of her profound statements sink in. Her words left me with nothing to say. My tears were the only response I could make. When she came across the room to hug me, I told her, "That's one of the most special things you've ever said."

How a Deceased Child Affects Everyone

We've been talking about sick or disabled children and their siblings. But when a child dies, parents are thrust into a multiple-crisis dilemma. Not only are they dealing with the loss of their child, they're also struggling with how to offer care and comfort to the remaining children. In some cases they also have to deal with the grief of their own parents, who have lost a precious grandchild. It's therefore not unusual that the siblings have to cope on their own, since the parents just don't have the emotional strength to help them, at least not yet.

What Is the Impact on Parents?

Can there be any emotional pain worse than that of losing one's child? Yet because of this, parents commonly shut down and respond in silence and secrecy regarding the child's death. This leaves the remaining children feeling haunted by their deceased sibling. They feel they must seal up their feelings, positive or negative, toward their lost sibling. If they had an enjoyable and close relationship, that bond must stay buried. If they had ongoing, unresolved conflicts, those, too, must stay buried. The children end up grieving alone.

Why the silence? What are parents afraid to talk about? Usually it's blame, the shared feeling that they could have done something to prevent the death. Children, with their limited understanding and resources, wonder why they can't talk about it. They may conclude that their parents are angry at them and that the sibling's death is their own fault. This is especially true if the siblings didn't get along prior to the child's death. And so we end up with a situation in which the children *won't* talk because it would upset the parents, and the parents *don't* talk because it would upset the children. Everyone is busy protecting everyone else. But this kind of protection brings no healing.

If the child who died was the favorite, the parents may not allow the deceased child's name even to be mentioned, in an effort to prevent damaging comparisons with the other children. Most of us saw the perfect example of this in the heart-wrenching film *Ordinary People*. Buck was the firstborn who could do no wrong. He died while sailing with his younger brother, Conrad. After Buck died, the mother became cold and unloving toward Conrad, while the father maintained only a superficial relationship with him. Conrad soon discovered he could never be what his brother was, and he struggled with his mother's comparisons of the two boys.

You see, Conrad lived in a home where his brother's memory was dominant, and his own hurts and angers were denied expression. His guilt intensified; he failed in school and eventually attempted to take his own life. He finally found the help he needed, not in his family, but in a psychiatrist who helped him unlock his feelings, face them, and grieve in a healthy way.

When a sibling dies, it increases the surviving child's sense of vulnerability to death. His emotions run the gamut from being sad to being worried about who will care for him and watch over him to being pleased that he could be the center of attention now.

What does this jumble of feelings create in a child? Often it's guilt and confusion. And a parent's response is so important. Parents may minimize their involvement with a remaining child because of their own grief. But remaining children need to be given the opportunity to express all of their feelings.

What Is the Impact on Siblings?

Many factors may inhibit a child's ability to grieve the loss of a sibling. These are some of the most common obstacles:

- Parents have difficulty grieving past or current losses and have not provided a model.
- Parents are unable to handle their children's expressions of emotional pain.
- The children worry about how the parents are handling the loss and try to protect them.

- The children are overly concerned with maintaining control and feeling secure. They may be frightened or threatened by their grief. The feelings may seem too intense.
- The children do not have the security of a loving, caring environment.
- The parents do not caringly stimulate and encourage the children to grieve.
- Surviving children may question their role in the death. Misplaced guilt is further enhanced if they have ambivalent feelings toward the deceased sibling.
- The family fails to acknowledge and discuss the reality of death or other loss.

One of the crucial struggles for young children is reconciling what they know about death (for instance, it only happens to old people) with the death of a sibling or playmate close to their age. That's why so often a young child will talk about the "should haves." They may say again and again, "I should have…"

Help them finish the statement. It could be "I should have stopped him…; I should have helped him…; I should have told him…"

One mother found her son saying, "I should have…" over and over again. She asked, "I should have *what?*" He recounted a list of "should haves," all indicating that he should have protected his brother more.

His mother said, "I understand, Danny. Daddy's got the 'should haves.' Mommy's got the 'should haves.' We all have them, and it's all right to have them. It's okay to know that all of us could have done something different and would have, if we had the choice."[6]

Birth order once again seems to have some significance in how children handle these situations. Older children feel more guilt over having wished their younger sibling would disappear, while younger children feel more of a burden to replace the deceased child.[7] Some adult siblings take it upon themselves to try to fill the hole in their parents' lives by constantly being available or even trying to emulate their dead sibling.

Many siblings end up competing with the child who died, especially if their parents glorify the deceased child's abilities, intelligence, or goodness. When the surviving children hear about their wonderful dead sibling, they may feel unloved or even jealous. They may feel it's an impossible task to compete with the memory of a dead sibling; this in turn leads to resentment, which leads to guilt.[8]

And what about fears? Children who lose a sibling can experience a number of fears, including:

- Fear of losing you, other siblings, or grandparents. They tend to see the remaining people as candidates for death.
- Fear of their own death, especially if they were younger than a sibling who died, and they're approaching the age at which he or she died. If there was a disabling accident, they may become concerned about health as they approach that age.
- Fear of going to sleep, because they equate sleep with death. Even the prayer "If I should die before I wake…" reinforces this misconception. Dreams and nightmares intensify the fear.
- Fear of separation because of the perceived insecurity of the home and family. They're hesitant to talk about their feelings because they may upset other family members.

Several other factors impact the lives of the surviving children. Consider, for example…

What was the intensity of the death? If a child actually sees a brother or sister die, it may bring on lasting trauma. Consider the impact of a child's discovering a sibling floating facedown in a swimming pool or seeing a sibling struck by a car.

What is the role of imagination? Even if the death occurred else-where, what actually happened to their sibling is left to their imagination. This could lead to denial of the loss.

What was the length of time in dying? When a sick child takes years to die, the other children feel helpless, abandoned, and put on hold because parents have had little time to devote to the well children. These kids have also assumed many of the parental chores around the house.

What is the level of false guilt? The remaining children feel they could have done something to keep their brother or sister from dying. Many children thus live with guilt, self-blame, and even the haunting question, "Why do I deserve to still be here?" They also may feel that they somehow caused their sibling's death.

Amid all these painful situations and aching questions, there is much hope for the grieving family. Remember, no one can provide a quick cure for loss and grief. You, as a family, must make your own unique pathway through the pain. I invite you to remember that with grief, as with any crushing adversity we face in life, the best way *out* is always *through*.

Chapter 6

The Grieving Family: Roles, Rules, and Responses

We've seen that a family is a complex mechanism of various actions and reactions. Each person makes his own contribution to the special mix that becomes uniquely "my family." As a result, each family ends up with a personality all its own. Some call it a family system.

Like a ship sailing into heavy winds, that system sometimes gets tossed around, buffeted, even severely damaged. It flounders off course or loses its trim, especially when it sails headlong into devastating loss. Yet every family likes things to remain on an even keel. If a family is prepared and skillful, it can adjust to the threatening conditions. It can make the moves necessary to keep everything in balance, even as it's weathering the worst of times. Is your family like that?

These families don't ignore the pain or try to circumnavigate it.

They don't try to forget the past or leave it behind.

They don't even "overcome" their grief, since it will always be a part of their life together.

So how does a family keep the balance? We can observe some typical ways these families successfully navigate through grief to reach their new state of equilibrium. For one thing, they realize that their members will take on differing *roles*. They also learn what to expect when it comes to family *rules* and *responses* in crisis. Most important, they're able to adopt survival *attitudes* based upon principles that have stood the test of time.

DISCERNING THE DIFFERING ROLES

What keeps your family in balance? It's each person doing his or her part, pulling the load and contributing. Because everybody has a role to play.

A family needs the support of individual members. If one person experiences a loss, crisis, or trauma, there will be a change of balance. If a child fails a grade or is discovered using drugs, he won't respond as he usually does. Somebody in the family will have to pick up the slack in order to get the family back in balance.

If a family member dies, or is disabled and can no longer do what he's supposed to do, this creates other losses within the family. If your child breaks his arm at school, this loss (of mobility, self-care, ability to play Little League baseball, do chores, do homework, practice the piano, etc.) impacts every other family member and disrupts the accustomed roles and routines. That is, other family members are recruited for his roles and routines, which takes them away from their own routine and adds work to their lives. The family system has changed, individual responsibilities have changed, and relationships with one another have changed.

My point is this: *Healthy families know this will happen, they antici-pate it, and they move forward with this new way of life for as long as it takes.* More attention and help will now be given to the child with the broken arm. Tasks and chores will be reassigned to others. It's difficult, and there may be some complaining, but all of this has to happen to ensure that the family continues to function.

Has your family experienced this kind of transition yet? If not, you will in some way in the future. If a parent becomes ill and incapacitated, often a child or all the children have to fill in with some adult roles. If roles aren't filled, the family functioning is thrown out of kilter. This often happens in a death, divorce, or chronic illness.

It can all work quite well. The downside is that sometimes roles aren't assigned suitably, which creates serious consequences. What if a child is given a role that's inappropriate, such as expecting a daughter to take on her deceased sister's personality or asking an eight-year-old boy to be the man of the house now that his dad is gone?

Beware of such assignments. A new role can hold multiple gains... and severe losses.

What Are the Rules Around Here?

Along with roles, every family has rules. Some are accepted and encouraged while others are rebelled against. For our purposes, the key question is this: What are the rules in your family about *feelings?* In some families, if a member continues with so-called unacceptable feelings, he or she may be rejected by the others. And so a split in the family system opens up.

Typically, some of the rules about feeling and acting are clearly stated while others are only implied. Either way, break them at your own risk! The following list shows some of the more common rules in dysfunctional families. Do you recognize any of them in your current family or your family of origin?

A Few Rules in the "Out of Balance" Family

Here are some of the things parents often "tell" their children. These rules come through whether in spoken words or in the general atmosphere and ordering of family interactions:

- You must make me happy.
- Don't get excited (or angry, sad, fearful, etc.). Such emotions threaten to unblock my own tightly controlled feelings.
- Your job is to take care of me.
- You will be loved if you perform up to my standards.
- Walk on eggshells.
- Keep things orderly and calm around here.
- Live in denial.
- Don't speak the truth if it will make any of us feel bad.
- We must not openly grieve our dead loved ones; it's too painful for us.
- We must not touch one another. It could lead to problems.
- If you need something, I'll give it to you. I know your needs better than you do.[1]

It's when losses hit that some of the most longstanding and cherished rules are finally forced into the open. So take a look at your family's expression of feelings. Read the list on page 92, and circle those feelings you are personally comfortable with. Underline those that are difficult for you to experience and/or express or to observe others expressing. Place a check by those you observe in your child. For those you don't see your child experiencing or expressing, what might be the reason? *Is there a rule in place here?*

afraid	guilty	hurt
angry	frustrated	excited
confused	embarrassed	dejected
lonely	anxious	happy
sad	ashamed	elated
depressed	discouraged	isolated

(Suggestion: Ask other family members to answer the same questions, and discuss your responses. Keep in mind that our children will probably express the very feelings we have never resolved in our own lives.)

Remember that when we grieve, we may hold our emotional pain in our bodies in the form of muscle tension. Drs. Joseph Biuso and Brian Newman have developed a Feeling-Tension Inventory. See page 93 for a part of it.

A healthy family, and one that recovers sooner, allows all its members to know, have, and express their feelings in an appropriate manner. Instead of seeing this as a problem, they look at it as an opportunity for all of them to grow and to grow closer. Only in giving and receiving from one another our truest and deepest feelings do we grow in intimacy.

Sometimes family members do indeed have the same feelings but express them at different times—even months apart. As one mother said, "It would have been so much easier if we had been in sync with our feelings. But each of the three children hit the anger stage at a different time. It was as though there was a balloon of anger floating through our home for months." It takes a toll on parents as they juggle their own feelings while they help a child process his or her feelings, which often change from day to day. You wake up the morning after a day of anger expecting more of the same—only to find depression and quiet withdrawal.

The goal is to reach a new state of balance in your family. If the rules are restrictive and burdensome, it becomes more difficult to do so. If the rules are aired and pared down to acceptable levels for all, then you can begin working on your new way of life together. You'll need to ask questions like these:

- Will we continue to participate in the same recreational activities? What new things will we do?
- Will we all keep going to the same places as we used to—or has the meaning changed too much?
- Will we still feel comfortable with our family and friends? What things can we do to help develop a new level of comfort?

A Feeling-Tension Inventory

Pause for a moment, take a couple of deep breaths, and begin checking out your body:

Where do you sense tightness, discomfort, or pain?

Place your hand down by your abdomen and breathe. Get a sense of what you are feeling down in that area. Are you unsettled, not at peace?

Put your hand over your heart, and just allow yourself to feel what's going on in your heart. Are you tender-hearted? Heavy-hearted? Is your heart aching?

Place your hand at your throat and along your jaw muscles. Are you swallowing back hurt, anger, sadness, fear? Are you clamping down on your feelings? Do you wish to "snap" back at someone or "bite their head off"?

It is good to take time regularly to ask ourselves: Where is the anger in my body just now? the hurt? the sadness? the fear?[2]

- Will we find it difficult to "fit in" with other intact families? (Where does a family who lost a child fit in? Where does a family who lost a parent fit in? Now that the divorce is final, where are other divorced families we can connect with?)
- Will we stay in the same house, or will we need to downscale or to move? What will help make these changes easier on us?

With regard to moving, one young father said: "We lost our home, and now we're renting. We can't invite our friends over. We're embarrassed, and so are the kids. And we can see it in the faces of others. They're not sure they want to be around us."[3]

GET READY FOR UNIQUE RESPONSES!

It's easy for us parents to try to set the record straight so that every family member will respond to the missing one in the same way. After all, it would be easier to handle a significant loss in the family if all the members were on the same page with their grief. But within a family, every person has his or her own history with the one who's missing. Others' perceptions of the missing person and their memories may be quite different from yours.

Sometimes others assume that each family member has lost the same relationship. This may not be true. They have not lost the same person— the person who was a certain way with and for them, a unique relationship. And each family member might respond to this unique loss in a different way.

Instead of trying to set the record straight, try listening. Listening and reflecting may help your children sort out fact from fantasy, sort out the way he or she *wishes* it had been compared to the way it really was.

The point is, *you can't expect a child to respond the way you do.* But your child will learn from you by watching you grieve. This is another opportunity for you to teach your child about grief. Remember, in order to meet your child's needs, you need to take care of yourself and your child. Out of your strength (even in the midst of your own grief), you can assist your child.

You want to draw closer, but there is even a danger to all the closeness that occurs. It's supportive, but it could also make family members prone to blame or to get angry and impatient with each other. One may start blaming everything and everyone possible...except himself. This could be a child or even a parent. He feels the pain of the loss, but you don't see it. Here are some other possible responses:[4]

A family member announces, "This isn't anything we should talk about again." She attempts to control everyone in the family by imposing a universal gag rule. She blocks others in their expressions of grief.

Another says, "Of course you can talk about it—but not with me." Members in this family may grieve, but they end up doing it alone.

Another may be responding to everyone who asks, "We are doing just fine, just fine, but thanks for asking." Yet the child and others may not be doing fine!

Another may respond with anger: "This is just one more thing we have to deal with! Why do things like this always happen to this family!"

Another responds with shallow platitudes: "Oh, let's not be sad about this. Our faith is all we need, and it's going to see us through." There is truth in this, but if sadness isn't allowed, the grief is buried, waiting to erupt someday. This is a form of denial.

Another doesn't say much at all, but her body does all the talking for her. Her grief is absorbed into her body, and medical symptoms soon begin to appear—headaches, backaches, hypertension, skin rashes, nervousness, indigestion.

Just imagine a child who has experienced a major loss and hears these various responses from his mother, father, older siblings, and extended family members. What is he to believe about grief? How is he to act?

You can be the one to help him.

Snapshot of Survival: A Top Seven List

How can families adjust to their losses…and survive? Each family is unique in its specific coping responses; however, we can identify some key characteristics of the surviving family. This "top seven" list offers a quick summary.

1. Surviving families learn from others who've made it.

2. Surviving families express their emotions in healthy ways, recognizing that tears are a gift from God that don't need apology.

3. Surviving families look for solutions rather than create a war zone of blame.

4. Surviving families don't magnify their problems, nor do they get stuck using victim phrases, such as these:

> I can't…
> That's a problem…
> I'll never…
> That's awful!
> Why is life this way?
> If only…
> Life is one big struggle.
> What will I do?

5. Surviving families don't allow themselves to become bitter, refusing to live in the past or to focus on "the unfairness."

6. Surviving families resolve their conflicts. New conflicts aren't automatically contaminated by a reservoir of past unresolved issues. (If a family hasn't learned to resolve conflicts *before* a crisis, it's not likely to do it *during* one.)

7. Surviving families cultivate a biblical attitude toward life.

In this survival list, each item is important. But I want to stress the final one, the one that should really go at the top of the list: cultivating a biblical attitude.

Top of the Survival List: Attitude

Why is attitude so important? It's because some crises you know you will experience in life, but other crises take you totally by surprise. That's when you face the crucial decision about how to interpret the event. In a very real sense, your interpretations *are* your world.

Have you been there? I have. So many events in or near my life I never anticipated.

I never expected that an office next to mine would be blown up by terrorists, with people injured and killed. But it happened.

I never expected a business associate to mismanage the running of my business to the extent that I would almost lose that business. But it happened.

I never expected that a high school boy on one of my outings as a youth director would fall over a four-hundred-foot cliff to his death. It happened. I watched as they carried him out in a body bag on a horse.

I never expected that my daughter, at the age of twenty, would take a detour in her Christian life and live with boyfriends, use cocaine, and move into alcoholism. But it happened and continued for four years.

I never expected to have a son born profoundly mentally retarded with brain damage and then suddenly die at the age of twenty-two. But it happened.

As we've faced these crises and losses over the years, my wife and I have relied upon many passages from God's Word. One passage in particular came alive as we depended on it more and more:

Consider it pure joy, my brothers, whenever you face trials of many kinds, because you know that the testing of your faith develops perseverance. Perseverance must finish its work so that you may be mature and complete, not lacking anything. (James 1:2-4)

The *Amplified Bible* says,

Let endurance and steadfastness and patience have full play and do a thorough work, so that you may be [people] perfectly and fully developed [with no defects], lacking in nothing. (v. 4)

We've found that learning to put that attitude into practice is a process. The passage does not say, "respond this way *immediately.*" We apparently have to feel the pain and grief first, and then we'll be able to consider it all joy.

What does the word *consider* mean? As I studied in commentaries, I discovered that it refers to an internal attitude of the heart or mind that allows the trial and circumstances of life to affect us either adversely or beneficially. Another way James 1:2 might be translated is "Make up your mind to regard adversity as something to welcome or be glad about."

In other words, you have the power to decide what your attitude will be. You can say about a trial, "That's terrible. Totally upsetting. That's the last thing I wanted for my life. Why did it happen now? Why *me?*"

The other way of "considering" the same difficulty is to say, "It's certainly not what I wanted or expected, but it's here. There are going to be some difficult times ahead, but how can I make the best of them?" Don't deny the pain or hurt you might have to go through, but ask, "What can I learn from this? How can I grow through this? How can I use it for God's glory?"

The verb tense used in the word *consider* indicates a decisiveness of action. It's not an attitude of resignation in which you say, "Well, I'll just give up. I'm stuck with this problem, and that's the way life is." If you resign yourself, you will sit back and do nothing.

Instead, James 1:2 indicates you will have to go against your natural inclination in order to see the trial as a positive. There will be some moments when you'll have to remind yourself, "I think there's a better way of responding to this. Lord, I really want You to help me see it from a different perspective." Then your mind will shift to a more constructive response.

This often takes a lot of work on your part. Discovering the truth of the verse in James, and many other passages like it, will enable you to develop a biblical perspective on life. And that is the ultimate survival tool. Again, it takes time. The greater the loss, the worse the trauma, the longer the recovery will take.

Thankfully, God created us with both the capacity and the freedom to determine how we'll respond to the unexpected tragedies life brings our way. We wish that a certain event had never occurred, but we can't change the fact that it did.

The point is, I can always choose my attitude, no matter the circumstances that come crashing in. I think of the Viennese psychiatrist Viktor Frankl, who spent most of World War II languishing in a Nazi concentration camp. He suffered all kinds of humiliating brutalities, barely escaping the gas chambers—though his father, mother, brother, and wife all died in the camps.

At one point he faced the fact squarely: Everything had been taken away from him. However, as he reflected on this over several days, he came to a new and even more powerful realization: I do actually have one thing left.

What was that one thing? It was his power to choose *how he would think about* what had happened to him. That was not taken away…and could never be taken. In fact, no matter what happens to any of us, we retain our ability to decide how we will respond.

> The experiences of camp life show that man does have a choice of action. There were enough examples, often of a heroic nature.… We who lived in concentration camps can remember the men who walked through the huts comforting others, giving away their last piece of bread. They may have been few in number, but they offer sufficient proof that everything can be taken from a man but one thing: the last of the human freedoms—to choose one's attitude in any given set of circumstances, to choose one's own way.[5]

Frankl's insights in the concentration camps became the foundation for a whole new approach to psychotherapy built upon "thinking right." We Christians can learn much from this approach as we turn to the Bible and encounter such encouraging words as these:

> What, then, shall we say in response to this? If God is for us, who can be against us?…Who shall separate us from the love of Christ? Shall trouble or hardship or persecution or famine or nakedness or danger or sword? As it is written:

"For your sake we face death all day long;
we are considered as sheep to be slaughtered."
No, in all these things we are more than conquerors through
him who loved us. For I am convinced that neither death nor life,
neither angels nor demons, neither the present nor the future, nor
any powers, neither height nor depth, nor anything else in all
creation, will be able to separate us from the love of God that is
in Christ Jesus our Lord. (Romans 8:31,35-39)

Finally, brothers, whatever is true, whatever is noble, whatever is right,
whatever is pure, whatever is lovely, whatever is admirable—if anything
is excellent or praiseworthy—think about such things. (Philippians 4:8)

According to the great spiritual writers of the past, all of life's blessings
come as a result of giving in and giving up—until we reach a blessed point
of acceptance. Listen to how C. S. Lewis put it:

Until you have given up your self to Him you will not have a real
self.… The principle runs through all life from top to bottom. Give up
yourself, and you will find your real self. Lose your life and you will
save it. Submit to death, death of your ambitions and favorite wishes
every day and death of your whole body in the end: submit with every
fibre of your being, and you will find eternal life. Keep back nothing.
Nothing that you have not given away will ever be really yours. Nothing in you that has not died will ever be raised from the dead.[6]

In the midst of your hurt and confusion, can you remember that a
marvelous resurrection awaits you? So much that you have lost will be
restored by infinite multiples. The first and most difficult step, though, is

to accept what is, *just as it is.* Circumstances never fully work out the way we want them to be.

But circumstances will change. And within God's will and in His time—here or there—they will surely change for the better.

> Then I saw a new heaven and a new earth, for the first heaven and the first earth had passed away, and there was no longer any sea. I saw the Holy City, the new Jerusalem, coming down out of heaven from God, prepared as a bride beautifully dressed for her husband. And I heard a loud voice from the throne saying, "Now the dwelling of God is with men, and he will live with them. They will be his people, and God himself will be with them and be their God. *He will wipe every tear from their eyes.* There will be no more death or mourning or crying or pain, for the old order of things has passed away." (Revelation 21:1-4, emphasis added)

Chapter 7

It's Different for Them:
A Look at Age Differences

M r. Wright, I'm not sure I can tell whether my child is grieving or not. It's been several months since his brother was lost in Afghanistan. It's hard for Jimmy to grasp the fact that Ed is 'missing.' If he were dead, we would have closure. I guess it's hard on all of us. Are there any signs I should be looking for?"

I've heard this type of question countless times. Why? Because as an adult, you may have some idea of how adults grieve. But a young child is different. A child in grief is a mystery. If you're looking for predictability, you may not find it. For example, your child might be visibly upset. If so, is it the child's own inner pain, or is he simply mirroring the behavior of the family? On the other hand, your child may not be upset—or perhaps just briefly upset—since he believes the problem will be remedied…

"We won't really move…"

"Sister isn't really dead…"

"Mom and Dad aren't really going to divorce…"

Or your child may act out in new or odd ways. Sometimes he or she is looking for attention. Some sulk or pout or get angry or belligerent. Some will talk incessantly, while others clam up. If the loss is a death, she may not want to go to the funeral or viewing, or if she does, she may ask question after question after question.[1]

Children are the forgotten grievers in our country. Therefore, we have trouble discerning what it looks like when they're in pain and mourning. Adults seem to receive all the attention while children get left out of the equation.

But children not only grieve; their grief is unique. We need to know what to expect.

What Can You Expect?

It's one thing to help your child work through the typical childhood losses that all children experience. But I assume your child has also experienced the death of a close friend, classmate, or family member, and that is the reason you're reading this book. When you understand what is a normal response for the age of your child, you'll know how to help him or her through the process of grief. I'd like to use two different scenarios, involving variously aged children, to help set the stage for what you can anticipate.

Scenario: When an Uncle Suddenly Dies...

Imagine a family with a beloved favorite uncle named Phil. He keeled over suddenly while eating his third bratwurst at the family's annual Fourth of July picnic. Everyone panicked, shouting for help, while two of the brothers threw Phil into a car and rushed him to the hospital. However, there never was a chance to save Uncle Phil. He had suffered a massive heart attack. What effect does this have on the various nieces and nephews?

Jimmy is two and a half years old. He's at the age of helplessness. Uncle Phil had spent a lot of time with Jimmy, so he, too, feels this loss. Not only that, Jimmy feels unprotected because some of the consistency of his life has been taken away.

Mary is four, and she has her own beliefs about death. She thinks it's temporary and reversible. Uncle Phil is dead today, but he'll be home tomorrow. And she also thinks she'll never die (what she sees in her favorite cartoons reinforces her thinking). For her, and others her age, death is similar to taking a trip from which you return. Mary tells her mother she wants to call or send Uncle Phil an e-mail. This is her attempt to continue some kind of relationship with him.

Mary sits down and draws some pictures to express what she thinks about death. She draws heaven, which is filled with angels and clouds. Many children at this age draw underground vertical boxes with people inside. Drawings of either type reflect the belief that a person's life goes on in the body, either above or below us, in death.

Mary isn't joking when she asks how Uncle Phil will get his favorite fishing magazine each month. What type of thinking is this? It's concrete and literal, which is what every three- to eight-year-old engages in.

John is seven. His beliefs about death are different from Mary's. He knows that when you're dead, you're dead, but he doesn't believe that he himself will die. This is how he's similar to a preschool child: He thinks he's immune. But he wants to know if death is contagious. *Will life still be safe for me?*

If John sees Uncle Phil's body, he'll ask question after question. He may ask you if you will ever die. How would you answer this question?

You could say, "Everybody dies someday, but most live to be very old." Behind his question may be a deep concern over his own safety.

John may ask if he can have Uncle Phil's pocket watch, since he won't be using it anymore. He may ask:

"How did he die?"

"Did he *know* he would die?"

"When he's in the casket in the ground, can any bugs get in?"

"If he's going to be buried, why is he all dressed up?"

Get ready for an onslaught of questions. Seven-year-olds want details. Some want just one sentence filled with facts; others want a full-length story. Be glad he asks you, because if he doesn't, the person he'll be asking is himself...and he doesn't have the answers. Giving him answers will help him deal with the underlying feelings he may not share.

John also needs to talk about what you may think is unmentionable. I know some parents who have invited such discussions with statements like these: "Sometimes you may have a question you're afraid to ask. Whatever it is, you can ask, and we'll work on finding the answer." Remember, they do want to talk about the unmentionable.

Scenario: When a Classmate Has a Terrible Accident...

Little Kaisha was running and playing on the school playground at recess. She never saw the big delivery truck swerving toward her over the sidewalk. The vehicle, driven by a man with a great deal of alcohol in his system, never slowed. Little Kaisha fell under its huge wheels in an instant.

Most of the other children on the playground saw everything that happened, along with Mrs. Harris, the third-grade teaching assistant. She quickly ushered all the children into the gymnasium while school administrators called for an ambulance and the police.

What about the other kids?

Fred, a six-year-old, keeps asking Mrs. Harris questions like these:

"I didn't see Kaisha after she got hit. Was there a lot of blood?"

"What did her head look like?"

"Were her eyes closed?"

You may not want to talk about these things, but the child needs to. Knowing some of the details provides him with a sense of relief. Talking with him factually is far better than letting him create a multitude of horrendous details in his own imagination.

Justin, an eleven-year-old, also witnessed the accident at the playground. His main question is, "Did her family have any insurance?"

When the child becomes a preadolescent (nine to twelve), he will probably have an adult understanding of death. For him, death is permanent and irreversible. Everyone will die.

He will tend to intellectualize his losses. He'll seem to become overly clinical with some of his questions and comments. Sometimes his questions and concerns are so factual you wonder if he has any feelings at all. He does, but he wants to stay in control. And so seemingly inappropriate questions, comments, and even jokes will flow. It's Justin's way of coping.[2]

DIFFERENT AGES, DIFFERENT RESPONSES

These two scenarios hint at some of the characteristics of grief you'll see at various age levels. Now let's get more specific about those qualities by breaking down the age levels in greater detail. You'll notice that I'm deliberately overlapping the ages, because there is no set time at which every child's thinking and coping abilities move into the next developmental stage. Children reach certain emotional and cognitive stages amid age *ranges*. So be ready to apply my generalized descriptions to the child you know best: yours.

Unique Features of Childhood Grief

In general, a child grieves differently from an adult. Instead of experiencing ongoing and intense distress, a child is likely at first to deny death, then grieve intermittently for many years. Other features include the following:

- Grief comes out in the middle of everyday life. It can't be predicted.
- A child can put grief aside easier than an adult. One question may be about her grandfather's death; the very next question will be about her doll.
- Grief comes out in brief but intense "episodes."
- Being limited in verbal expression, a child expresses his grief in actions.
- A child often postpones her grief—or at least part of it.
- A child's grief often lasts *throughout* childhood; pieces of it last into adulthood.

Infant to Toddler

Remember that grieving occurs even in infants. Children between four months and two years of age express distress when responding to a loss. At this stage, even separation from Mom is felt as a significant loss. If the separation is sudden, the child will express shock and protest. Prolonged separation creates despair and sadness. The child loses interest in toys and activities that are usually pleasurable. Unless a caring individual steps into the vacated role, the infant will become detached from everyone.

Ages Two Through Five

Children between two and five years old may show their grief in a number of ways. Because they don't understand the significance of the loss, they may ask seemingly useless questions again and again and again. They may ask, "Hasn't he been dead long enough?"

For children at this age, comprehending concepts takes time, and the idea of death hasn't been fully formed yet in their minds. They may seem bewildered and tend to regress in their behaviors, even becoming demanding and clinging. If what was lost is not returned, expect expressions of anger to increase.

An adult may need to help the children identify, acknowledge, and express feelings of loss. Many adults make the mistake of removing children from familiar surroundings after a family death or trauma. This further undermines their sense of security and raises their anxiety levels.

In the case of death, children at this age are obsessed with thoughts of the lost loved one. They become overwhelmed by an intense sadness. A toddler doesn't yet understand how a death is any different from going away on a trip. Their thinking and reasoning capacity are just developing. It may still be hard for them to distinguish between themselves and someone else.

Their sense of who they are and their sense of safety depend on the presence of, or feedback from, another person, especially a parent. So if a child loses a parent at this age, *his entire world collapses.* After all, look at what a parent does. A parent holds the child's life together, directs him, protects him, gives him treats, buys him things, and is the ultimate provider. A child tends to idealize this person and dwells on reviewing and remembering what they had together.

In other words, young children focus on themselves. Often they fail to take into account the viewpoints and beliefs of others. They engage in their own private language and frequently talk past each other. They're unable to distinguish between themselves as the speaker and someone else as the listener. It's all blurred. They also assume their words carry more meaning than they actually do and have little concern as to whether the listener understands or not.

At this age, children are literal and concrete in their thinking. Until this type of thinking begins to change around seven years old, they can easily be confused by statements like:

"Don't pull my leg!" (Is somebody hurting you?)

"That's a bunch of baloney." (I'm hungry.)

"Keep your shirt on." (I didn't take it off.)

"Don't give up the ship." (Where's the boat?)

"Hang in there, kid." (Mommy hangs up pictures, but…)

Young children often make their own unique connections. They tend to group objects, events, and people together in a way that makes sense to them but to no one else. For example, Tom's grandfather had a stroke while they were sitting together at a baseball game. Now Tom becomes anxious whenever he visits the neighborhood playground because it's next to a baseball field. His parents, though, don't understand what's wrong with him.

These parents need to know that a preschool-to-kindergarten child has a unique way of approaching life. He can build an amazing world around something that is not real—without seeing any contradiction. It doesn't bother the child if his perceptions are inaccurate. His understanding of death is limited. He knows it's related to sadness, but a death doesn't

Obstacles to Grieving?

Can you identify what things may actually *inhibit* your child's abilities to grieve? Consider the following factors:

- The family fails to acknowledge and discuss the reality of death or loss.
- The children are worried about how the parents are handling the loss and attempt to protect them.
- The children are overly concerned with maintaining control and feeling secure and may be frightened or threatened by the grief.
- The children don't have the security of a loving, caring environment.
- The parents have difficulty grieving past or current losses.
- The parents are unable to handle and accept their children's expressions of pain.
- The parents don't caringly prod, stimulate, and encourage the children to grieve.[3]

arouse an emotional reaction per se. He has his own way of trying to make sense of the upheaval of a loss.

One example was the four-year-old and two younger siblings who were trying to make sense of it all at their mother's funeral. They said good-bye to their mother at home, right after she died. The eighteen-month-old seemed to understand at some level and had said, "Bye-bye. Mommy all gone." But at the funeral service, the children kept running to the coffin and kissing her and then looked back as they ran back to their seats. And each time this happened, they looked disappointed. It appeared they were trying to see if their mother, like Snow White, would wake up with a kiss. Adults tried to explain this was different from Snow White, and the children looked dejected as they struggled to make sense of this information.

Ages Three Through Seven

As we've seen, children between the ages of three and seven years old engage in *magical thinking.* They believe their own thoughts can influence people and events. For instance, a child who is upset about a parent taking a trip may wish the car would have a flat tire so the parent won't leave. If the parent is killed in a car crash caused by a blowout, the child feels responsible.

The magical thinking we're talking about is the inaccurate conclusion that a child reaches about a loss experience. Usually it's that he is responsible for what happened. Thus, he takes on a need to fix it.

A child makes inaccurate conclusions because of her limited cognitive ability. When a child engages in magical thinking, it diverts her from healthy mourning. Her thinking sounds like this:

A seven-year-old girl is sick. This sick girl hugs her grandfather when he comes to visit. Her grandfather has a heart attack and dies. This girl concludes, "I was sick and touched Grandpa, and he got sick and died. It is my fault that Grandpa died." This girl later concludes that if she is perfectly good, grandfather will come back, which initiates a pattern of behavior driving her to be compulsively good.[4]

Children engaged in magical thinking tend to draw three types of conclusions. Watch for these:

1. Children active in destructive magical thoughts may believe they have the power to be responsible for the loss.

   "I got sick, and I touched Grandpa, and then he got sick and died."

   "I heard them arguing about me, so it's my fault that my parents divorced."

2. Children with magical thoughts may believe that they have the power to fix the loss.

   "If I have the power to kill him, I have the power to bring him back to life."

   "If I can get my parents in my counselor's office together, they will stay married."

3. Children with magical thoughts may believe that they can eliminate grief and the process of mourning for themselves and others.

   "If I am perfectly good, my sad feelings will go away."[5]

This is an age when fears increase. Children become aware of threatening events in the world around them. They're curious about bodily functions. When they experience the death of a loved one, children may ask questions like these: Can he still eat? Can he go potty? Does he cry? Will he get out of the box and hug me again? Will he be a ghost?

Children this age don't understand the permanency of death. For them, it's reversible. E.T. came back from the dead. So did Jesus and Lazarus. And so does the coyote in the roadrunner cartoons. If you wish hard enough, a person will come back to life.

When a pet dies, young children may act as if it is still alive by calling it, asking to feed it, or looking under a bed for it. These kids see people and animals as if they are cartoon characters—able to survive anything. To them, death is merely a deep and temporary sleep. Parents often reinforce this misconception by telling them the dead person is "resting" or "just didn't wake up." Even some of the terminology used by funeral homes reinforces the denial of the permanency of death. For example, you may be led into "the slumber room."[6]

Children in this age group often focus their attention on one detail of an experience and ignore everything else. They have difficulty seeing the whole picture clearly. Thus they don't comprehend the *significance* of loss. If Grandpa dies, they may ask or think:

"Does this mean someone else is going to die?"

"Grandpa died from a headache; Mommy says she has a headache too."

"Old people die. Daddy is very old. Daddy might die too."

Be prepared for indirect questions aimed at finding out if someone else might die: "How old are you? How old is Daddy?" You must explain the difference between

- very, very sick…and just "sick"
- very, very old…and over twenty
- very old and very sick…and very old and *not* sick[7]

As children get older, they do develop the ability to understand loss and even death. Yet then they become especially vulnerable because they can grasp the significance of their losses, but at the same time they have limited skills to cope with them.

If there is a death, they often look on it as a "taker," something that comes and gets you. The question, "Who killed him?" is common. They may accept death as a reality but not the fact that everyone is going to die. One of the worst prayers that has been taught to children (including me) over the years was "Now I lay me down to sleep. I pray the Lord my soul to keep. If I should die before I wake, I pray the Lord my soul to take." What damage does this do to young children?

Children also hide their feelings at this age because they "don't want to look like a baby." Afraid of losing control, children may vent their feelings only when alone. To others they may appear insensitive, uncaring, and unaffected by the loss, leaving the parent unaware of the extent of their grief. At this age, children need to be encouraged *again and again* to vent their feelings. Allowing your children to see you grieve and talking about your own feelings can help them work though their feelings.

Finally, remember that, in order to cope with the loss, these kids live in a fantasy world of their own making. Morbid thoughts are common. In an effort to maintain the preexisting relationship with whatever or whomever they lost, these children engage in fantasy. They tend to idealize the qualities of the loved one, and other members of the family don't fare as well when compared to their fantasies.

Ages Five Through Eight

Five- through eight-year-olds may experience a variety of feelings ranging from misplaced guilt to embarrassment about being in some way different from their peers. They often feel pressure to be strong and self-reliant. This is brought on by their fear for themselves and concern for other family members. They may become more helpful than usual in order to shut out the pain of their loss and feel more in control.

Early-elementary-age children begin to reason sequentially. Therefore the understanding of death becomes more specific, factual, precise—and more matter of fact than emotional. As they progress, they become more curious about death, funerals, and burials. And they don't see any contradiction in talking about positive results when there's been a death. Jimmy said, "I know my sister died; I miss her. But Mommy and Daddy have more time for me now."

This type of statement may bother adults but not the child. He may describe the death of a family member or pet in a very factual way, even while becoming aware of his own vulnerability: "I will die sometime too."[8]

Ages Nine Through Twelve

Children between the ages of nine and twelve years old experience dramatic changes in their thinking processes. They are now developing *conceptual thinking* and *problem-solving skills.*

Toward the end of this stage, they also move from *concrete* to *abstract* thinking. Children who are beginning to think abstractly relate more to real-life people and events than to a fantasy or a make-believe world. They begin to understand the meaning and ramifications of loss. If the loss is a death, they are now able to reflect on the consequences of death, and that's evident in their questions. They may ask:

"What will happen to Frieda now?"

"Who will take care of her grandfather?"

"Will Bill have to move now?"

Even though their thinking is more developed, they do jump to conclusions. They don't always understand what they hear, especially if it's communicated to them in adult terminology. Adults need to communicate clearly to these children, using simple statements, repeating and rephrasing important points of the message.[9]

If you don't talk to your children, they'll talk to themselves and fill in the blanks. Imagination—and other children—are not good resources for getting the facts straight. Here's why communication with your children is so important:

- It tames fears. By talking with them about death and grief, you can recreate a secure place so they can learn to trust the world again.
- It gives a sense of control. Children feel confused and besieged by new emotions. They need to be anchored by adults—especially you.
- It gives permission to express feelings. Children don't grieve on command; they need the freedom to come to us at any time, knowing we're open to communicating.

- It prepares children for future losses. Most adults have never been prepared for this. A sheltered child can't cope as well as those who understand the truths of life.[10]

These children are becoming more independent, but they are still fragile. In fact, they may exhibit some of the same responses as their younger counterparts. They struggle with feelings of helplessness and childishness but don't want others to know, so they often put up a facade of coping with their losses. They recognize the finality and irreversibility of losing someone or something they love. Thus, as in every stage of life, they need to grieve over the loss.

Part III

Helping Your Children to Grieve

Chapter 8

Think Their Thoughts

Ted was only twenty-seven months old when he began waking up several times a night, screaming hysterically for a bottle of sugar water. It went on for weeks. At one point his father became quite firm with him and told him he wouldn't be getting any more bottles at night—and to go to sleep.

But something about the way his son cried caused Dad to stop and return to the crib. He lifted the boy up and asked him, "What will happen if you don't get your bottle?"

The little boy was still tearful and sniffling. He said, "Can't make contact."

The father was puzzled. "What do you mean, Ted?"

"If I run outta gas," said the little boy, "then I can't make contact—my engine won't go."

The father recalled a recent family outing when the car had run out of gas. So he asked, "What are you afraid will happen if you run out of gas?"

His son began to cry and said, "My motor won't run, and then I'll die."

Now Dad remembered when he'd sold an old car. A buyer tried starting the engine, but it wouldn't turn over. In the ensuing conversation, the little boy heard statements like these:

"It's probably not making contact."

"The motor died."

"I guess the battery's dead."

Was Teddy putting this all together in his mind?

Dad asked, "Are you worried that if you run out of gas or food, you'll die like the motor of a car?"

"Uh-huh."

"Well, Ted, a car has a key, and we can turn it on and off at any time, right?" Then his father said, "Now, where is your key? Is it your nose? Is it your ear? Is it your belly button?" Teddy laughed. "Can I turn your motor on and off? No. You're not like a car at all. I can't turn you on and off. Mother can't. No one can. Once your motor is on, it stays on. It's on when you're awake and when you're asleep. Your motor runs all night long, and you never have to fill it up with gas. Do you understand now?"

"Yes."

Teddy had been putting other concepts together too. He'd overheard his parents talking about how a brother got "gas" from drinking sugar water. Earlier Teddy's parakeet had died, and Dad gave this explanation: "Every animal has a motor inside that keeps it going. When something dies, it's like a motor stopped running. That motor just won't run anymore."

Look at all the different pieces of information Teddy pieced together to explain death! To this child it all made sense.[1]

———◆———

Clearly, as we see from the case of Teddy and his dad, the things we say and the stories we tell can have effects we never imagined. So we need to soberly ponder two important questions: How do children *think* about death? How do they *feel* when it occurs? These are the twin themes of this chapter.

A Child's Thoughts Are Not Your Thoughts

Children think like...children. Why shouldn't they? One five-year-old girl was told that her uncle's cancer was like a seed that grew and grew in his body. Her parents never noticed that from that time on she never ate another seed. Not any kind of seed. When she was many years older, someone said, "I notice that you never eat any seeds. In fact, you pick them out meticulously. Is there some reason for that?"

"Well, don't you know?" she said. "If you swallow them, you die." All those years she'd held on to her childhood belief. It would have been helpful if someone had noticed when she was young and asked her, "What will happen if you eat that seed?"

When you tell a child, "Your dog went to dog heaven," it may be a quick, satisfying answer for you and the child. But is it accurate? And what kinds of childlike thinking will it trigger?

An adult woman remembered that when she was a preschooler, her favorite old dog had to "go away for a long sleep." And that's what she believed for years. When she reached adolescence, she finally realized her dog wasn't away napping. He had died. But since as a little girl she had thought the dog was just "off napping," she had given him a casual good-bye. Now, in discovering he was dead, she was angry that she hadn't given him a proper send-off, with a meaningful memorial service.

A four-year-old was told that his father was in heaven, "right up there somewhere." He went and immediately told his mother his daddy was on the roof. To him, "up there" meant real high, as high as the top of the roof. Some parents tell their children Santa Claus is up on the roof as well. It's a simple transition for a child to believe his daddy and Santa are up there together, the best of friends.

A three-year-old's friend was killed, and his mother told him that Jesus came and took him to heaven. His response was, "That's not a very nice thing for Him to do. I want Billy to play with me. That's not nice for Jesus to come and take away my friend."

Obviously, before offering pat answers and seemingly nice solutions, we need to ask ourselves, "If I do explain death in this way, how will it end up in the child's understanding?"[2]

BEST POLICY: THE SIMPLE TRUTH

When we're not clear how a child will think about what has happened, we might get a little queasy about dealing with the topic at all. Will we just cause more confusion and pain? That's why too often we want to protect the child with "nice" explanations. Or we choose to believe he can't handle what really happened; therefore, we just clam up.

We must courageously force ourselves into the opposite approach: Children need to be told the truth in a way they can comprehend. We tell them, "Uncle Jim has gone to sleep for a long, long time." No, he didn't. Uncle Jim has died. Why inject a fear of sleeping into a child's mind?

"Uncle Jim went away on a trip." This isn't true—and do you really want to instill a fear of going on trips or plant the seeds of abandonment?

I've heard so many explanations for death that are not only untrue but damaging. No doubt you've heard some of the "classics" too:

"God wanted your mother to help Him in heaven."

"Your baby brother is a singing angel in heaven now."

"She was too good for this world. God wanted her in heaven."

And we wonder why a child begins to misbehave (he wants to stay here with you, not be whisked away)! It's better to say, "She died because she had a disease called AIDS," or "He died because he was riding his bicycle and ran into a car."

It's so much better to learn to use truthful death language with your child. "We lost him" is a common phrase when someone dies, but to your child he is not dead. Little Jimmy will want to go out and look for the person you lost. Avoid "he is away" concepts.

If it was an illness, distinguish between a minor and fatal illness. Your child will learn that other children die, but you can reassure him that it is only when a child is *very* sick, has a terminal illness, or has a serious accident that he or she dies.

What you say and how you say it sets the stage for the thinking-and-feeling responses of your child. That's because you, as the parent, hold great power in the child's life. If you listen closely to your child's questions and make sure your answers are thorough but appropriate for the child's intellectual development, then you will be a great help. Your candid way of talking and your openness to emotional expression will point the way for your child's responses.

One more reason why telling the truth is so important: Loss heavily impacts children's theological beliefs. What they believe about God (rightly or wrongly) undergoes radical change. We call this a crisis of faith.

Questions never before asked now arise. If answers aren't truthful or accurate, the child experiences yet another loss: trust in adults.

How Will You Handle the Funeral?

What happens when it comes time for making the final arrangements? The thoughts, feelings, and behaviors of children vary at this time, and they continue to be strongly influenced by the reactions of the surviving family members as well as other adults.

In the very helpful little book *Thank You for Coming to Say Good-bye* by Janice L. Roberts and Joy Johnson, funeral director Dan Schaefer wrote a section titled "And Then There's Jack":

> Kim's children had done well with their first visit to their grandpa's viewing at my funeral home. They brought gifts, a small doll, and an action figure Tommy knew Grandpa would like. They wanted the bottom of the casket opened to make sure Grandpa's legs were there. (In my experience, 80 percent of the children want this assurance.) They counted the prayer cards and flowers, checked out the sealing mechanism on the casket, and things seemed to be going well.
>
> Then Kim said, "Something's bothering them." She asked, and they replied, "Why can't Jack say good-bye to Grandpa? He loved Grandpa and Grandpa loved him." Jack was an eighty-pound German Shepherd. We decided Jack should visit.
>
> The children walked Jack into the viewing room, and together we helped them lift him up to see Grandpa. The children placed Jack's paw on Grandpa's arm. These children had done what was important. There are many children and adults who are not given the opportunity Jack was given.[3]

What opportunities do children need when a relative dies? As you formulate your answer, keep in mind these four pertinent guidelines:

1. Children can be given a choice about whether to attend the wake, funeral, or burial. Yes, give your kids the option. Certainly, it can help them if they're included in the rituals of saying good-bye. Viewing the body and being at the memorial and graveside service will raise a few questions, but it will also answer others. So we give our kids choices regarding the funeral.

But these need to be *informed* choices, with children prepared for what they will see and experience. Children should be told what is going to happen and what they are going to experience.

In preparing children for the funeral, fit the following explanation around your family's plans and special traditions:

_____ will be taken from _____, where he died, to the funeral home. At the funeral home _____ will be dressed in clothes that he liked and put into a casket. A casket is a box we use so that when _____ is buried, no dirt will get on him. Because _____'s body isn't working anymore, it won't move or do any of the things it used to do. But it will look like _____ always did.

People will come and visit us and say how sorry they are that _____ died. After _____ days the casket will be closed and taken to the church, where people will say prayers for the family. Then we will go to the cemetery where _____ will be buried in a place that _____ picked out.

If you like, you can come to the funeral home and visit for a while—even go to the cemetery. You could bring something to leave with _____ if you want. That would be nice.

We have to go to the funeral home to make plans, and we'll let you know all about them when we come back. We will be gone _____ hours.

For cremation, use this additional information:

After we leave the funeral home, _____ will be taken to a crematory, a place where his body will be turned into ashes. Then we will take those ashes and _____ (scatter them; keep them in an urn). Since _____'s body doesn't work and doesn't feel anything, being cremated doesn't hurt.

Tell the children what will happen, then give them the choice of going or not. Often the thought of a funeral home is frightening. It's one thing to watch horror movies on television and another to take that first step through a real door. Fears can be alleviated if a child has a structured tour, can ask questions, open and close doors, etc. Children take field trips all the time to fire stations, factories, music centers, and libraries. But I wonder if a funeral home has ever been on the list?

2. Including children in the planning of the funeral has a positive effect. Children who are prepared for a funeral are better able to handle it than those who aren't given prior information. It helps them to feel important and useful at a time when many are feeling overwhelmed.

When children are involved in the service, whether it's for a parent or other family member, let them express themselves in their own way. They may want to bring the person's favorite food and share it with everyone. They may want to place some of their own items or gifts from the person (or their own special possessions) in the casket. One little girl brought her aunt's favorite hat to put in the casket, while her brother brought a picture of himself. Children may draw a picture to put in the casket.

3. Children who are involved want the funeral to reflect the life of the relative. They prefer hearing about real-life actions, events, and memories rather than focusing on the loss itself or on the afterlife. In addition, if the dead person's body has significantly changed because of illness or accident, it's important to describe some of this change. ("It's still Grandpa, but you know he was sick and lost a lot of weight, so he will look thinner...")[4]

4. Visiting the grave helps children remain connected with the loved one. It's important to have a relationship with the dead relative, especially a parent. This is part of the continuing process called "constructing." The constructing process involves discovering the meaning of this loss rather than just "letting go" of their relative; this discovering continues to be a part of the children's life experience.

With the loss of a parent, there's a huge vacancy in their life now. This is a time when they are working through what place the deceased parent has in their current life.[5] Children who have remained connected after the loss are better able to talk about the dead parent. They can talk to family members as well as others.

GET READY FOR THE QUESTIONS

The problem is that many adults don't know what to expect, are uncomfortable with what they encounter, and struggle with answering the questions streaming from their children, especially since magical thinking in children will likely produce some pretty far-out questions! How would you answer the following?

What is a casket? A casket is a special box made out of metal or wood, and it's used for burying a dead body.

Other questions to expect: "Can you breathe in a casket? What if they want to get out? How do they go to the bathroom in there?"

What is a burial plot? This is where we bury the body. We call it a grave. We bury the casket deep in the ground so no one can bother the remains, and they can stay there. Some people are buried in buildings called mausoleums. Some people prefer to place their loved ones in the buildings rather than in the ground.

Other questions to expect: "Does the ground get them dirty? Are there worms and bugs in there? What happens when it rains?"

What is a cemetery? It's a place where many dead bodies are buried.

Other questions to expect: "Are they buried lying down or standing up? Do they all know each other? When do they get to go home?"

What is cremation? It's when the body is turned to ashes. But they don't really burn the body. The body is placed in a large ovenlike structure, and it's so hot the body dissolves into ash and small bones.

Other questions to expect: "Does it hurt? Does the body smell? What do they put the ashes in, and what do they do with them?"

What is a funeral? A funeral is a time when the person's friends come together and usually have some kind of service with a minister. Those who attend come to say good-bye, to honor the person, to share their favorite stories about the person, to comfort and support one another. We remind ourselves that, as Christians, the person's life may have ended on earth, but it's just starting with God and Jesus in heaven.

Other questions to expect: "Why do some people cry and some don't at the funeral? Why do some people laugh and some don't at the funeral? If the person is already in heaven, can he hear us at the funeral?"

What is a funeral home? This is the place where bodies are kept and prepared for the funeral. The funeral director takes care of all the arrangements, and this helps the family.

Other questions to expect: "Does he touch the dead body? What do you mean, 'prepare the body'?"

What is a hearse? It's a car that carries the casket with the body in it to the cemetery.

Other questions to expect: "Can we ride in the hearse? Is it spooky inside the hearse?"

What is a wake? A wake is a time when friends and relatives come together to celebrate the life of the person who died. There's usually food, and people tell lots of stories. There's a feeling of sadness and joy.

Other questions to expect: "Why do people laugh when they're sad? Do I really have to go to this?"

What is a viewing? A viewing is when the body is placed in the home, the church, or a funeral home. The casket is usually open there so those who come to pay their respects can see the person one last time.

Other questions to expect: "Can you touch the body? Does the person look normal? Does she smell?"

Will I have to keep going back to the grave? You may *want* to go sometimes, maybe when you're older, because it will help you remember the good things about the person and his or her life with us.

Other questions to expect: "Billy says we have to go back and visit the grave and put flowers on it. Do I have to go? Uncle Jim is dead. He won't know if we come or not, right?"[6]

While grieving, our children look to us for hope and encouragement. When they ask us questions, we need to avoid giving them platitudes and, instead, let them know it's all right to ask *why* when bad things happen. We need to admit to them that we don't have all the answers but that we'll get through it together. One mother told her six-year-old, "I know it is a sad time for you. We are all sad and wish things were different. There are many changes happening right now, but in time things will settle down. Someday the pain will go away. It may go away gradually and keep returning again and again, but as we help and love one another, it is going to go away."[7]

When you experience the death of a family member or friend, ask yourself if this is your child's first experience with death. If it is, your child will need your help to understand the loss and sort out his or her feelings about it. Be especially sensitive to the child's reactions and anticipate the unexpected from them. Use words and phrases the child can easily understand. It may help to rehearse with someone else what you plan to say.

Always be clear and as factual as possible, telling the truth about the

Answering Questions About Death

Dan Schaefer, author of *How Do We Tell the Children?* offers examples of how to respond to common questions children ask about death.

- "Will Grandpa ever move again?" (No. His body has stopped working.)
- "Why can't they fix him?" (Once the body stops working, it can't start again.)
- "Why is he cold?" (The body only stays warm when it's working.)
- "Why isn't he moving?" (He can't move, because his body isn't working anymore.)
- "When will he come back?" (He won't. People who die don't come back.)
- "Is he sleeping?" (No. When we sleep, our body is still working, just resting.)
- "Can he hear me?" (No. He could only hear you if his body was working.)
- "Can he eat after he is buried?" (No. A person eats only when his body is working.)[8]

death and what caused it. When kids ask questions, give them accurate information such as, "Your brother's heart stopped beating, and that is why he died." As I've stressed elsewhere, it's much better to use proper death language, such as "Grandpa died," rather than "Grandpa went to sleep." But be sensitive about how many details you give. If you have no answer to their questions, say so. Let them know, though, that when you do, you will share it with them.

In her book *Helping a Child Understand Death,* author Linda Vogel suggests that when parents are questioned about death, they tell their children something like this:

> We miss Grandpa, but we can be glad Grandpa doesn't hurt or feel sad anymore. His body is in the ground. Grandpa is with God, and we believe God will love him and care for him in a way more beautiful and wonderful than we can imagine. When people say Grandpa is in heaven, this is what they mean.[9]

———◆———

As we close this chapter, remember: Your marriage and your other children don't have to be secondary casualties of the original loss. You can take steps to strengthen your marriage and family life, and then you'll have a greater source of strength to draw from as you confront the issues facing you. As your family works, plays, and worships together, you will discover a healing comfort in these relationships. And be sure you allow the other family members to minister to you as you minister to them.

Chapter 9

Feel Their
Feelings Too

You're a young child. You live with your parents and siblings in a home with a big backyard, several large trees, and plenty of lawn for running and playing. You have several friends, but your best friend is Corby, a small mixed-breed dog. He loves to play with you and share your food (much to your mother's dismay). He tries to sneak into your room to sleep on the bed, and he listens to everything you say.

One day you decide to put him on your lap while you swing from one of the tall trees. Up and up you go, higher and higher, and it's great fun. But you lose your grip on Corby, and he plummets off your lap, twenty feet to the ground, bouncing off the hard base of the tree. You stop and run to him, but he's dead of a broken neck.

You stand there in shock. You think, *No!* but no sound comes out of your mouth. You want to cry, but you can't. You feel numb. You feel stunned. Your mother is crying, and your siblings are upset. But you're just numbed and stunned. And Mom wonders: "What's wrong with him?" "Didn't he care enough for his dog?" "Is he abnormal?"

It's hard enough for us adults to talk about death and the reasons for the terrible thing that happened. After the shock and numbness, we feel bad, we hurt, we want to avoid the pain. If it's this way for us, what is it like for a child?

In the previous chapter we attempted to think like children think. Can we do the same with feelings?

Assuming you've already learned to mourn your own losses of the past—and are continually involved in that process—you are well qualified to explore what children feel in their crises of loss. Consider, then, a child's emotional reactions to a serious loss such as death. We'll focus specifically on the anger, fear, and guilt that come crashing in...after the shock.

ANCHORED IN ANGER?

What do you know about anger? What do you believe about anger? *Anger* is a controversial word as well as an emotion. It affects all of us but baffles children and parents alike. Some children express their anger like heat-seeking missiles. There's no warning. Everything has been calm, and then your child explodes in rage. With grief it's especially unpredictable. Or your child's anger may be stealthy. Like a submarine attack, it suddenly sneaks into your discussion.

In any case, remember that anger is a warning sign, a clue to underlying attitudes. It's designed to help us detect improper and potentially destructive attitudes. It may be the first emotion we're aware of, but it is rarely the first emotion we experience in a particular situation. The emotions that most frequently precede anger are fear, hurt, or frustration. Not only are they painful, but they also drain us of energy and increase our sense of vulnerability.

Here's the point: At an early age *many of us learned that anger can divert our attention from these more painful emotions.* So we could speak of at least three causes of anger. First, *hurt* causes anger. When I'm facing rejection, criticism, or physical or emotional pain, a very normal reaction is anger. I strike back and counterattack what I perceive is causing the pain. In fact, it doesn't take any of us long to learn that it's easier to feel anger than pain. If I get angry, I can avoid (or at least minimize) my pain from hurt. Anger provides an increase of energy and can decrease my sense of vulnerability. Perhaps I can even influence or change the source of my anger.

Second, *frustration* causes anger. A child expects something or feels entitled. When it doesn't work out, that frustration transforms into anger. He's angry because he believes his future has been dramatically changed; he won't be with that special person anymore. He feels victimized by events that are out of his control.

Children may direct frustration-anger at their parents

...for not telling them that the person who died was so sick.

...for spending so much time with the sick person. They feel neglected and isolated.

...just because they need someone to be angry at.[1]

Children may express this anger in different ways. It may be targeted like a well-aimed rifle bullet or sprayed in all directions like shotgun pellets. It may be directed at family members, friends, teachers, pets, or even at God. It may be expressed in tantrums, fights, silent hostility, or verbal blasts. As difficult as it may be to experience these demonstrative expressions of anger, realize that it's a healthy sign. The alternative response—bottling up all this anger—can result in digestive problems and depression.

Third, *fear* causes anger. The child feels defenseless, thinks the worst will happen, feels powerless, overwhelmed, and anxious. None of these are comfortable feelings! And perhaps, if he's angry, whatever is causing the fear will go away.

Most children and adults don't want to admit they're hurt or afraid. Others could attack or ridicule them, so they camouflage their pain and vulnerability with anger to protect themselves. But I've seen parents teach their children to say, "Mom or Dad, I'm hurt-angry," or "I'm afraid-angry," or "I'm frustrated-angry." (Do you think you could learn to do that in your family? It's worth teaching your child to talk with you like this.)

Anger tends to push others away or elicit defensiveness; we're more drawn to the expression of the other emotions. However, when your child displays anger, you could try responding with something along these lines:

"Tell me about your hurt…fear…frustration. I'd like to hear about that."

"It sounds like something is really bothering you. I'm wondering if you're frustrated about something or feeling hurt or perhaps afraid. Could you tell me about it?"

"I'm wondering if, along with your anger, you might be feeling…"

What you're doing is getting at the cause, or source, of the anger: the hurt, frustration, and fear. It's worth a try, right?

Children express anger in a variety of ways that you can watch for: stubbornness, halfhearted efforts, forgetfulness, not hearing, laziness. Your child may act confused, pretend she doesn't understand, or be overly clumsy, "accidentally" breaking things on purpose. All of these expressions can be very irritating, but you will know what's going on. What, specifically, can you do to help your child with anger?

1. Keep current. Help your child to deal with each hurt as it arises. Allowing hurts to accumulate makes them seem overwhelming, a mountain of hurts that cannot be moved.

2. Reinforce responsibility. Your child needs to take responsibility for his own anger. The anger belongs to him; no one else is making him angry. The anger may or may not be appropriate, but it exists, and it must be reckoned with.

3. Teach two-sidedness. Teach your child to allow other people to have feelings also. Anger is seldom one-sided; others have a right to feel angry. Help your child see both sides of the conflict: "If Billy has hurt you, it's possible that it's because you've hurt him, too."

4. Constantly converse. Listen to, receive, and accept your child's anger. Talking about anger helps to pinpoint its source and also may diffuse its intensity. Once your child is aware of where the anger came from, encourage her to let the anger go and focus on dealing with the cause of the hurt.

5. Focus on forgiveness. Show your child how to forgive. Explain why revenge is dangerous. Remind your child of what she would want if she were in the other person's shoes. And model forgiveness yourself.

6. Consider confronting. In some cases, you may want to show your child how to face up to the person who is doing the hurting. Of course, this isn't always appropriate or even possible; the person may be too manipulative or reactive and may have moved away. But where possible, encourage and support your child in "facing up to the enemy."[2]

We've seen that one of the causes of anger is fear. So here I'd like to delve into one of the common childhood fears a little more deeply—a particularly distressing one for young children: the kind of fear that goes bump in the night.

FEELING THE NIGHTTIME FEAR?

Fears exist during the day but especially at night. Children's minds can run wild as they lie in bed and as they sleep. Darkness can be frightening, because it generates fears of being isolated, left alone, or being lost. Children need to know it's all right to talk about their fears. Suggestion: You might try gradually reducing the amount of light in their rooms at night. Also, share with them Proverbs 3:24,26, and help them commit it to memory:

> You will not be afraid when you go to bed, and you will sleep soundly through the night.... The LORD will keep you safe. (TEV)

If your children struggle with nighttime fears, here are some ways you can help them overcome:

1. Help your children know it's all right to be afraid—and to talk about it. Everyone has fears, and a certain amount of fear is normal; we certainly don't have to be ashamed when we're afraid. You might talk about some of your own childhood fears and let your children know that those fears eventually passed.

Sharing about their fears helps children keep fear in perspective. If you know the extent of their fear, you will be better able to help them overcome any distortions they have. Many parents have found it effective to invite their children to draw their feelings on paper, act out their fantasies, or use puppets to talk about their fears.

2. Let your children know it is also normal NOT to be afraid. Help children observe another person *not* being afraid in a situation that scares them. They begin to see the possibilities of courage as the fearful object or event shrinks in size.

3. Help your children understand that being afraid is temporary. Will they indeed be afraid forever? No. Give them a message of hope for the future, which will in turn create an expectation of success.

4. Help your child learn a new response or behavior to replace his fear response. These are called counterbehaviors or fear-replacing behaviors. Encourage your child to imagine himself not being afraid in a situation that would normally frighten him. Positive imageries are powerful substitutes. Participating in a positive activity or favorite pastime during a fearful situation can eventually lessen his fear.

5. Help your child articulate. Sometimes children are afraid but have difficulty actually stating what they're afraid of. Maybe they're too upset or don't have the verbal skills to adequately express themselves. It won't help to try forcing it out of them or shaming them into telling you. Your best approach is patience and continued observation. You may find it helpful to keep a log of the times your children are afraid. By making comparisons, you may discover a pattern that will identify the source of their fears.

Counselors often use picture books, allowing children to point to whatever they're afraid of. Or children can use dolls to act out situations. You might also try a sentence-completion approach. You make up a sentence but leave the ending unfinished so the child finishes it for you. Here are some examples:[3]

- "Sometimes I'm afraid if…"

- "The thing that always scares me is…"
- "I feel afraid when…"
- "I remember a time when I was really afraid. What happened was…"
- "One thing that really helps when I'm afraid is…"
- "When I'm afraid, I need my parents to…"
- "One way I know God is with me is…"
- "The best thing for me to do when I'm afraid is to…"

As with adults, so it is with children: *Repeatedly facing our fears is the best method of overcoming them.* We need to teach our children to tap the creative powers of their God-given imaginations to see themselves handling their greatest fears.

Do not be afraid, for I am with you. (Isaiah 43:5)

GOING THROUGH GUILT?

With many childhood losses, children end up feeling guilty. It's difficult to identify all of the sources of guilt, but there seem to be three main reasons children experience guilt when loved ones die:

They died because I did something wrong. I misbehaved! Children have a knack for remembering things they've done that they think were wrong. They may have made a mistake, broken something, or forgotten to say or do something. Just like adults, children can end up with an incredible list of if-onlys.

I wanted them dead. I thought it, and it happened. It's important to remember that young children believe they can actually make things happen by thinking them. It's easy for kids to think their anger or aggression killed the loved one. Because they take on this responsibility, they live in fear of being found out and punished.

I guess I didn't love them enough. It's common for children to believe that if you love people enough, it will keep them from dying. They long for a second chance to make things right.

You understand cause and effect better than your child, who may be doing some magical thinking. For example, Jimmy's struggle is common among children. He would get angry at his brother, Phil, from time to time. He wished Phil would go live with his grandparents. He wanted Phil to leave him alone and quit picking on him.

One day Phil *did* go away. Permanently.

A car ran into Phil's school bus, and Phil died. But Jimmy felt responsible. He began saying things like, "I wish I hadn't…" and "If only I…"

When you hear regret statements, they're usually tied to guilt. If you suspect your child is experiencing guilt, you might ask, "John, do you ever find yourself thinking, 'If only I had…' or 'I wish I could have…'?" Offering such prompts—and then listening carefully—could help your child express his self-tormenting statements.

Along with regret-guilt is another form rarely talked about: relief-guilt. Adults and children experience this. Jean's younger sister, Becky, had been sick for five years. Naturally, Becky was the focus of the family's attention. Jean often felt left out—left with the leftovers. When Becky died, Jean was sad…but also quite relieved. After all, she wouldn't have to share her parents anymore, and she would get the attention she'd been wanting. But her relief carried a load of guilt with it. The more relief she felt, the more guilt she felt.

Finally, some children equate guilt with punishment. Here is one adult's recollection of her childhood experience:

When I was seven, my baby sister died of SIDS. Immediately I thought it was because of something I did. I also believed when you were bad, disobedient—call it whatever you want—you should be punished. When no punishment came, I began to act in ways that would cause my parents to punish me. I can see now that I just added to their fears by being out of control. But it was the only way I could get the punishment I thought I needed so I could feel better.[4]

How Can I Encourage the Feelings?

Naturally, you'd like to help your child share his feelings. Let me suggest several approaches. One is to use the Ball of Grief with children who can read. Ask them to identify the words that apply to them.

Grief…a Tangled Ball of Emotions

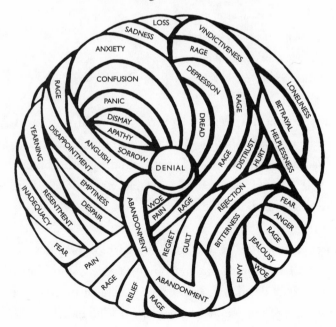

Another way of approaching feelings, especially when this is uncomfortable for the child, is to talk about feelings using the Five Fingers of Feelings. You could say…

Let's use our fingers to help us know what we're feeling. Adults and children often have five important feelings (hold up one hand, with your fingers spread out, and move a different finger for each feeling). There is a finger for sad, one for mad, happy, scared, and lonely. Let's see which of these you're experiencing. When you think about Grandpa not being here anymore, do you have (hold up one finger) a sad feeling? If your child nods her head, ask other questions like,

"Where is sad in our body?"

"What does sad look like on our face?" (Take some paper, and both of you draw a face with this feeling.)

"Does it have a taste?"

"When you're sad, what do you want to do?

"What would you like *me* to do?"

Proceed with each of the five feelings with your child.[5]

It may help at this point to have the child read you stories from a book like *Fears, Doubts, Blues and Pouts,* which I wrote with Gary Oliver. (This book can be ordered from Christian Marriage Enrichment by calling 1-800-875-7560.) Using stories or fables is a unique way to help a child discover and understand the cause for a loss in her life. Consider these stories.

The funeral fable. Let your child know you're going to share a story with him. In fact, both of you are going to create a story. For the child who understands death, you could say, "A funeral procession is going down a street, and the people who see it ask, 'Who died?'"

Someone answers, "Oh, it's somebody in the family who lives in this house."

"Who is it?"

Now the child continues with the story. If the child is so young that he or she doesn't understand death, say, "Somebody in the family took a trip and went far, far away. In fact, they went so far away they will never come back." (List the members of the family for this child.) An additional question you could ask: "Why would a person go away like this?" (Here you could bring in the Five Fingers of Feelings activity just described.)

The anxiety fable. "There was a child, and he was talking safely to himself. He said, 'Oh, I'm afraid.' What do you think he was afraid of?" (Additional questions: "What does being afraid do to us? Why are children afraid? What could we do about this fear?")

The news fable. This is a way to discover both the wishes and fears of a child. "A child comes back home from [school, church, visiting friends], and his mommy says, 'Sit down. I have something to tell you.' What do you think she is going to say? What's the expression on her face? What *don't* you want her to say? What would you *like* her to say?"

The bad dream fable. "Have you ever had a bad dream? Well, this child woke up one morning. He had slept all night, but he was still really, really tired. He said, 'Oh, I had a bad dream.' What was the dream about?"[6]

Humpty Dumpty. "Sometimes when you've lost something important—or a person—you feel like Humpty Dumpty. Remember him? He fell off of a wall and broke into a bunch of pieces. The king and his helpers couldn't help Humpty. They couldn't put him back together again. Sometimes we feel that way. But there is a difference. Our King is God. He loves us so much that He sent His Son to save us and put us back together better than we ever were. God understands your pain, too. Let's tell Him about each piece of your sadness, fear, and anger, and He will help you put your life together again."

> Blessed are those who mourn,
>> for they will be comforted. (Matthew 5:4)

Time of day. "What's the hardest time of the day for you? Sometimes remembering that Susie is gone hurts so bad in the morning that it feels as if you're being punished. David, a king in the Old Testament, felt this way too. He said, 'I have been punished every morning' [Psalm 73:14]. But God loves you so much, has so much compassion for you, that He wants your mornings to be better. And it will help you in the morning if you remember that the Bible tells us: 'His compassions never fail. They are new every morning' [Lamentations 3:22-23]. And David, who wrote the first verse we read, also said, 'Weeping may remain for a night, but rejoicing comes in the morning' [Psalm 30:5]."

Halloween. "When people lose someone they love and they're sad, sometimes they act like it's Halloween. You remember what many people do on that day, don't you? They wear a mask and pretend to be someone they're not. Part of the fun is fooling others into thinking you're someone you're not. Sometimes we do the same when we've experienced a loss and we're sad. People ask how we are, and we say, 'Fine,' when we're not. We put on a smile when we're sad. How can others help us when they don't know we're hurting? It's best to take off our mask and let others know how we really feel."

Never ending? "Do you wonder if your sadness will ever end? Sometimes I wonder when it will go away. I wish it would. This strange feeling we have is called sadness or sorrow. We'd like to wake up some morning and say, 'It's all better.' I would, wouldn't you? Well, it doesn't happen all at once. It happens a little bit each day. It's piece by piece. A month from now it'll be better, and three months from now it'll be better than that. And the Bible gives us hope that someday the sorrow will be gone."

Your sun will never set again,
   and your moon will wane no more;
the LORD will be your everlasting light,
   and your days of sorrow will end. (Isaiah 60:20)

Chapter 10

Help Them Get Unstuck

Often I hear parents ask:

"How will I know if my child is working through her grief all right?"

"How long should this take anyway?"

"How do I know if she's recovering...or if she's *stuck?*"

These are common questions, important questions. The main thing is not to put a timetable on your child's grief, because "recovery" is difficult to predict. And as the child progresses, remember that we all move forward a bit and then hit a bump in the road, move forward, hit another bump, etc. Though there are stages of grief, none of us follows the pathway to healing in thoroughly predictable ways. And sometimes a child can indeed get stuck in the grieving process.

What Does "Stuck" Look Like?

It's called *complicated mourning,* and I'll quickly list some of the signs before delving into one of them more fully:

Denial that doesn't change. Your child won't accept what has happened. He or she continues to deny that the loss even occurred.

Physical complaints that don't let up. You'll hear, "I have a headache, backache, stomachache, sideache," but even the family doctor can't find any cause for these complaints. The pains continue week after week.

Fear, guilt, or anger that won't subside. If these three emotions continue to undermine your child's life, it's time for serious concern. Explanations aren't alleviating guilt, and it's not just a matter of the child's age-related magical thinking. Ongoing or chronic anger that is "stuffed" results in depression. Depression can even lead to suicidal thinking and behavior.

Withdrawal that's universal. Sometimes a child will withdraw from one family member. But when he withdraws from *everyone,* he's telling you something important.

Personality that's dramatically different. Watch for significant changes in personality and behavioral patterns. Your child was outgoing but is now constantly withdrawn. She used to be gracious and encouraging but is now aggressive and sarcastic.

Eating and sleeping that's abnormal. Some children stop eating; others can't seem to stop feeding themselves. This isn't normal—nor is insomnia or constant sleeping.

Use that's abuse. An adolescent may attempt to deaden his pain by using drugs and alcohol as a means of self-medicating.

Regression that's overly dependent. Let's talk more about this one…

WATCH FOR UNHEALTHY REGRESSION

Along with the signs I've just listed, watch for regression. It's usually happening when parents are saying things like…

"Quit acting like a baby!"

"Grow up!

"I thought you'd stopped doing that last year!"

A child of ten wants to return to the security and sense of protection she felt when she was six. She remembers the structure and predictability. Taking on the behavior of those "good old days," she goes back in time.

What can you expect when this occurs? Your child will lean on you in every way, from the physical to the emotional. There's an overdependence. Even the delight of going outside to play can't pry her loose. She may not want you to leave for work or go anywhere that she can't go. If she was nursed or rocked as an infant, this, too, may be requested. You may wake up one night and find your child in bed with you or wrapped in a blanket, asleep, on the floor next to you.

The skills your child once mastered now seem to have vanished. You may be asked to tie her shoes, help her dress, or feed her.

School's not immune from these changes. Your child may act sick to avoid going to school or church. And when he's at school, he may have difficulty getting along with his friends. Not only that, you may get a note or call from his teacher because he won't work on his own in the class or because he's attempting to get individual attention. He leans on his teacher just as he's leaning on you.

Don't be alarmed by these responses. They won't last forever (although some behaviors may persist or periodically reappear for months or even years).

Your child needs support. What you're seeing are symptoms caused by the loss. It's your child saying, "I have needs too." Dr. Alan Wolfelt views these behaviors as indicating that the child's emotional needs are either not being met in a proper way or the adults may be trying to meet their own needs through their child's behavior.

He also suggests that grieving children have certain rights. They have the right to have their own set of feelings about the loss, to talk about their grief whenever they need to, to show feelings in their own way, to need others to help them, to get upset about little problems, to have unexplained outbursts of grief, to think about memories of the one they lost and…to move forward and recover.[1]

So I'm simply saying: Let your child retreat. Help her talk about her feelings. Or use play techniques to assist her in her grieving. Affirm, teach, and let your child know you love her, even in the midst of regressive behaviors.[2]

Help Them Get Unstuck!

Whether the loss is the death of a family member, a major move, or the loss of a pet, your children need permission to mourn. For certain children, permission may not be enough. They get stuck and need a special invitation to share their feelings as well as help learning how to express sorrow. A few sensitive, well-directed questions can often draw them out. If your children still cannot talk, don't force it. Just let them know that you are available and ready to listen when they want to talk. And you may want to look for other ways for them to express what they're feeling.

Once your children begin to talk about their feelings, it may seem like you've tapped into a gusher. They are, in their limited capacity, attempting to make sense of what has happened and regain their security. Children whose questions are answered, who are given a forum for discussion, have less need to fantasize and are much easier to help than nonexpressive children. If they don't share their feelings, watch for indirect questions or statements of concern, and try to put their feelings into words for them.[3]

Being available may be the most important element in helping your children get unstuck. Remember, they need affection and a sense of security in order to grieve. Touching them and making eye contact will provide comfort and reassurance. Let your children know it is normal to have ups and downs when grieving. They are not going crazy. Help them break the mourning into manageable pieces so they don't become overwhelmed. Using illustrations and word pictures can help them identify and talk about their feelings.

Following are some more ways you can help "unstick" them.

Give them opportunities for creative expression. Children who have difficulty verbalizing their feelings may find it easier to express them on paper. Drawing helps kids gain control over their emotional pain and eventually eliminate it. When the loss is a death, drawing is especially important, because it allows children to actually see what their feelings look like. That helps give them a sense of understanding and control.

Writing or journaling also helps with children whose writing skills are developed. It's easier for kids to express on paper the reality of what's happened, along with their fantasies about it. Writing a letter to the deceased person—or even to God—can do wonders. Encourage your children to read aloud and discuss what they've written. But remember to respect their privacy; the choice needs to be theirs.

Encourage them to express their thoughts, fears, and feelings creatively. For example,

- Draw a picture of Grandpa.
- Sing a song about Melissa.
- Write a letter to Dad, and ask Jesus to make sure he gets it.
- Write a book about Grandma.

- Tell Fido (or Dolly) about Justin.
- Help me remember what Fluffy looked like.
- Talk to God about Aunt Emily.

Create opportunities for playtime. Children may feel as if they're betraying the deceased if they have fun or allow themselves some enjoyment. But play is a normal and beneficial part of their lives; it gives them time to recuperate and realize that life goes on.

So periodically encourage your children to take a break from their grief and just play with friends. Play is an important form of expression for children, especially for younger children whose verbal skills are limited. In the safety of play, a child can vent all kinds of feelings. Play helps them regain a feeling of safety and security. It gives them a feeling of power over the effects of loss and allows them to separate themselves from what has happened.[4]

Dismiss their myths. It's important to discover whether your children are practicing magical thinking. Younger children are particularly vulnerable to this. For instance, your child may have argued with a friend who three hours later was killed in a car accident. Now your child may feel responsible. One young girl told her dog to "drop dead"—and the next morning it did! She thought she made it happen. Identify and correct such myths as soon as possible.

Allow your children to respond in their own ways. Don't expect your kids to respond as you do. Initially, they may not seem upset or sad. Young children may even have difficulty remembering the deceased. You may need to help them remember their relationship with the deceased before they can resolve their grief. Showing photos and videos will help, as will reminiscing about times spent together.

The important thing is to allow children to progress at their own rates. Just be available, or have someone else available, to observe their reactions. If they begin to express strong feelings, don't block them. Allow

them to cry or express anger or even bitterness. In time, they will probably begin to ask questions. Answer them simply and honestly, even
though you may struggle with them yourself.

Encourage children to continue their normal routines. It helps if
children continue certain family routines. Routines provide security, letting them know there are certain constants in their lives, things they can
rely on to stay the same.

One of the most practical things parents can do is to encourage their
children to take good care of themselves, to get plenty of rest and exercise,
and to follow a balanced diet. Basically, allow your children to live a normal life.

- Have them invite friends over.
- Let them spend the night with friends.
- Talk about it when they need to.
- Don't talk about it if they don't want to.
- Play with them; laugh with them; read to them; pray with them.
- Hug them.
- Laugh with them again.
- Hug them some more.[5]

BE READY TO BE FRUSTRATED

We need to watch our expectations, because we adults often have goals that
are inappropriate for our children's age level. I've overheard parents or other
relatives say, "You're going to have to take over now and be the man of the
family [or be the strong one]." This is an unrealistic expectation and places
too much of a burden on the child. These kinds of messages will short-
circuit the child's grieving process. So be careful to give age-appropriate
responsibilities.

Yet even when our expectations seem thoroughly reasonable and appropriate, we may feel as if our children still aren't "doing it right" for us. Then our own frustration can set in. As our children talk to us about a death, we may find ourselves frustrated for several reasons. Here are three common ones:

1. Your child may talk as though the person (or pet) is still alive. So you will need to remind him that the person is dead. And you might need to do this repeatedly. Naturally, what he asks or talks about could activate some of your own pain. You may wish he'd just keep quiet for a while!

But be clear about this: A grieving child will often try to re-create the former situation. It's his form of denial, or protest, and it can take various forms. For example, he may act as if nothing out of the ordinary has happened. One mother said, "I couldn't believe the way my daughter responded when her cat was run over. I expected her to come apart at the seams—or at least cry. But she just looked at me with no expression on her face at all. She seemed so uncaring, so unfeeling."

And at first many children respond in this fashion. It's normal. It's their Novocain. It's better than pain. It's their way of saying, "No. You're wrong. It didn't happen."

Don't be surprised if your child argues with you: "No, it wasn't our cat. He's out chasing mice or playing with his friends. It just looked like Tabby." Or he may say, "Show me it's Tabby. I have to see him." Children like to touch, see, or feel. (In some cases this may be advisable, whereas in others it may not be possible or even wise.) Protests may continue for some time.

Your child may attempt to re-create playtimes with Tabby. In time she will realize these attempts to re-create don't work, and this will actually remind her that "Tabby really is gone." And then she will have to fill that vacant spot in her life.

2. Your child may keep searching, searching, searching. Kids in grief may try to recover the lost loved one. They know it's not going to work, but they keep trying. This is particularly the case when loved ones are "lost"—missing in action, kidnapped, drowned at sea, or for some other reason the body is missing. Now the challenge becomes, can this loss be reversed? They think, *Maybe it's not really permanent after all!*

> When youngsters are convinced that retrieval is impossible, they may respond by trying to replace the missing person. They may begin to dress like, act like, or take over the roles and responsibilities of the person who is gone. They may become pseudo-mature caretakers or project personal concerns about safety onto other people or animals ("Poor puppy. Don't worry, I will take care of you"). Jealous of other families that are intact or feeling deprived (as they may very well be), they may set about trying to complete their family by urging their parent to remarry or to have another child.[6]

3. Your child will need to keep revisiting and regrieving. Even if you help your child through a difficult loss and you think he's worked through his grief, he will still need to revisit his grief years later. A friend shared with me that her son was nine when his three-year-old brother died after several months of severe medical problems. His mother took him to a counselor who worked with him for some time. The counselor said he appeared to be doing all right but that somewhere between the ages of fifteen and twenty-two he would possibly be affected by this loss again and need to regrieve. And at twenty that's exactly what occurred.

Regrieving is part of the developmental process in children. Maria Trozzi described the process with this example:

If a parent dies when a child is four years old, that child will continue to make sense of what it means not to have that parent as she grows and matures. As her needs for love and guidance for that person change, a child whose mother died when she is a preschooler will regrieve her mother's death through latency, preadolescence, adolescence, and adulthood. As her "meaning" of growing up without her mother changes, her grief will reoccur with each change. When she marries, gives birth and reaches the age at which her mother died, she also will regrieve her mother's death.[7]

Because of this regrieving, a child will grieve longer than an adult. The grief comes and goes...and sometimes comes again and again.

Part IV

Supporting Your Children in Special Circumstances

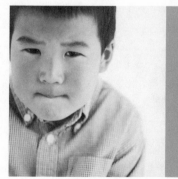

Chapter 11

Depression: When Feelings Get "Stuffed"

Kyle just isn't behaving like a healthy nine-year-old. He's been spending more and more time in his room, either lying on his bed or watching television. Every now and then he'll complain about being bored, but when someone invites him to play, he refuses. Whenever his parents say something to encourage him, he responds with, "Yeah, right. If you only knew."

What's wrong with Kyle? He's depressed. Yes, even children become depressed, especially if they've experienced a significant loss and pushed their anger inward.

Ashley is an active three-year-old (at least until last week). Now she just seems to mope around with a long face. She shows no interest, regardless of her mother's efforts to involve her in play. She's not ill; she just doesn't seem to care anymore.

Can toddlers become depressed too? Yes. In fact, even newborns can show signs of being depressed, although it's very difficult to diagnose.

How common is depression among children? I've seen research suggesting that as many as 8 percent of preschool-age children experience significant depression, and as they get older, their chances of becoming depressed actually increase. Most depression in childhood goes away quickly, but some children suffer from the more serious, disabling type of clinical depression as well. This chronic type seems to evolve for no apparent reason, or it is out of proportion to whatever apparently set it off.

The difficulty is that even concerned parents can be so distracted by their own marriage, occupations, or daily responsibilities that they miss the warning signs of their depressed children. They also fail to recognize the events that can trigger depression.

WHY DO CHILDREN BECOME DEPRESSED?

Many factors can trigger depression in children. Divorce remains the leading cause, coming, as it does, with a multiplicity of losses. Some of the other more common culprits are

- a physical defect or illness
- malfunction of the endocrine glands
- a lack of affection, creating insecurity
- a lack of positive feedback or encouragement
- the death of a parent
- divorce, separation, or parental desertion
- sibling favoritism
- relationship problems between child and stepparent
- financial problems in the family
- a sensitivity to punishment
- a move or change of schools[1]

Most of these causes center around loss, don't they? Children often become depressed because of a loss. Sudden loss is particularly hard on children, leaving them floundering and feeling out of control. On the other hand, a gradual loss they can prepare for is easier for children to manage.

Often depression is heightened if what is lost is perceived as necessary and irreplaceable. In his book on depression, Dr. Archibald Hart describes four different types of loss that can have a bearing on depression:

Abstract losses are intangible, such as the loss of self-respect, love, hope, or ambition. Our mind perceives these losses, and we may feel we have experienced them. These losses may be powerful and difficult to deal with because they're harder to identify.

Real losses involve tangible objects—a home, a car, a parent, a close friend, a photograph, or a pet. We could feel and see the object prior to the loss.

Imagined losses are created solely by our active imaginations. We think someone doesn't like us anymore. We think people are talking behind our back. Children often excel at this. Their self-talk focuses on negatives and may not be based on fact.

Threatened losses can be the most difficult to handle. This loss has not yet occurred, but there is a real possibility it will happen. To a child, waiting for the results of a physical exam or waiting to hear if he can go to his relatives' farm for the summer carries the possibility of loss. He's waiting for the hammer to fall. Depression occurs because the child is powerless to do anything about this type of loss. In a sense he's immobilized.[2]

Suffice it to say, if your child is sad or depressed, look for a loss.

What Are the Signs of Depression?

How can you know if your child is really depressed and not just appropriately sad about something that has happened? Clearly, we need to understand the difference between a healthy sadness and an unhealthy depression. The feeling of sadness is less intense than that of depression.

It doesn't last as long, nor does it interfere with day-to-day functioning. Depression causes us to function at 50 percent of normal, and this lower functioning intensifies our feelings of depression. That's a key sign.

A depressed child feels empty. He can't fully understand the meaning of life or what is happening within, but he knows something is wrong. Here's a composite of the depressed child—a depressive Top Ten List, if you will. Your child probably won't display all of these symptoms, but be on the lookout for several being exhibited:

1. Sadness and indifference. We call this apathy, and it can be expressed in several ways. He might appear restless but doesn't become involved in activity. He may decline to do things he usually enjoys, preferring to be alone or just daydream. Apathy in a child is a symptom of internal stress.

2. Withdrawal and inhibition. It's a listlessness. Your child may look bored or even appear to be ill. Some become mute; they just won't talk. A depressed child looks discontented and seems to experience very little pleasure from life. In addition, a depressed child looks for comfort and support from others, but when she receives it, she refuses to be comforted and encouraged.

3. Physical complaints. A depressed child may display physical symptoms, often complaining of headaches, stomachaches, dizziness, insomnia, or eating and sleeping disturbances. These symptoms are called "depressive equivalents."

4. Sense of rejection. Many depressed children feel rejected and unloved. They withdraw from any situation that may disappoint them. They fear and expect rejection and protect themselves from it.

5. Down on self with negative talk. When a depressed child speaks, she's negative about herself and everything in her life. She draws conclusions based on her negative mind-set rather than on fact. This further reinforces her feelings of depression. Depressed kids become overly sensitive, hard on themselves, and self-critical. They create unreasonable goals and blame themselves when they fail to attain them.

6. Frustration and irritability. A depressed child will show unusual levels of frustration and irritability. When your child fails to reach his goals, he'll be especially hard on himself, commenting disparagingly about his abilities and value.

7. Silly facade. Some children will mask their feelings of despair by clowning and acting foolish. Provocative children are less likely to appear in need of comfort and support, so the depression can continue undetected.

8. Up-and-down moods. Some children demonstrate drastic mood swings when depressed. One minute they appear to be up, and the next they're in the pit of despair. These children tend to believe that if they are "good enough" and work hard enough, life will turn around for them.

9. Being the problem. The depressed child may become the family scapegoat. His behavior may elicit anger, and parents might label him a problem child. With this label, the depression continues, and the child may begin to live up to his label.

10. Aggression or passive aggression. Some depressed children will become aggressive and obsessive in order to cope with how bad they feel. Or depressed children may tend to be passive, excessively dependent, and assume parents automatically know their needs. Since it's impossible to read their thoughts, their needs go unmet. They may become angry and respond in passive aggressive ways.

Obviously, depressed kids won't exhibit all of these characteristics. But when some of them exist, don't assume the child is merely misbehaving.[3]

Many children experience depression because they're having difficulties dealing with people. The strongest need a child has is to belong, to be part of a family and social group. Children who are having problems developing positive relationships are in crisis and can become depressed. Again, they've experienced a loss.

Depression can also result from a traumatic incident. In such cases, the depressed feelings are usually short-lived, and the child soon returns to normal. I've listed situations that may not be bothersome to adults but can cause temporary depression in children.

- Failing an exam or a class
- Being overlooked for a desired honor
- Performing poorly in an organized activity, such as Little League, T-ball, or gymnastics
- Unable to find someone with whom to play
- Being reprimanded or punished
- Arguing with a parent, sibling, or friend
- Losing a favorite object or a pet
- Being denied a request
- Entering puberty
- Moving from one home to another or losing friends

While these situations cause only short-term depression, circumstances that seem to have no end can leave a child emotionally drained and less resilient. Here are situations that can generate long-term depression in a child:

- Constant arguments within the family
- Obvious marital problems between parents
- Lack of one-on-one communication
- Frequent criticism
- Conditional love: affection and positive attention based on performance
- Financial pressures
- Substance abuse within the family

- Inadequate and inconsistent discipline
- Limited social and intellectual stimulation
- Difficult socialization with peers
- Lack of success caused by learning problems

A depression-prone child can interpret a parent's response as a reinforcement of his negative worth. For example,

- Frequent criticism
  Child's interpretation: "I can't do anything right."
- Lack of individual attention from parent
  Child's interpretation: "I'm not important."
- Harsh or angry words from parents
  Child's interpretation: "I make others feel upset."
- Parents' failure to acknowledge accomplishments
  Child's interpretation: "The things I do don't count."
- Parents focusing on negative or upsetting behavior
  Child's interpretation: "Everyone expects me to be bad."
- Parents' failure to keep promises
  Child's interpretation: "No one cares if I'm disappointed."

Over time, continuous negative experiences like these contribute to feelings of low self-worth, which lead to depressed feelings.[4]

How You Can Help Your Depressed Child

Most parents don't know what to do when their children are depressed. For example, what can you say to them?

Seven-year-old Katy would begin to cry at the drop of a hat. She constantly made negative statements about herself. She talked about being ugly (which was far from the truth), how others didn't like her (her friends called every day), and how she couldn't do anything right (she was a straight-A student). This had been going on for a month. No matter what her parents said or did, she seemed to get worse rather than better.

A good place for Katy's parents to start was by simply communicating that they care for her, want to be with her, and will be available to her.

Conveying acceptance is also important. There is healing in physical touch. An arm around your child's shoulder, a pat on the back, or holding your child's hand can communicate comfort and acceptance. But by all means, be honest and tell your child, "I don't really understand all that you're going through, but I'm trying—and I'm here to help you."

If your child's despair over her loss or trauma is overwhelming because of what she saw or witnessed, she may need to find a way to forget the experience. If so, you can expect to hear "I don't remember" or "I don't

Feeling Unimportant?

The method of expression differs from child to child, but depressed children feel they're less valuable than others. These feelings of inadequacy and low self-esteem may appear in the following ways:

Quitting a club or ball team because he sees himself as insignificant. ("They'll never miss me.")

Failing to reach out to help others for fear of rejection. ("She doesn't want my help.")

Rejecting affection because of a feeling of unworthiness. ("She can't really love me.")

Deliberately breaking rules because he thinks following them will lead to failure. ("Others expect too much of me. They won't like it when I fail.")

want to talk about it." Or she may change the subject or try to distract you by acting out in some way.

Or your child may not say anything at all.

Here are some practical guidelines to help you understand and deal with the problem of depression. How closely you follow them will depend upon the intensity and duration of the depression. If your child is experiencing short-term depression and still functioning, certain suggestions will not apply. However, if the depression has lasted quite a while, and your child isn't eating, sleeping, or functioning on a normal level, you will apply more of these guidelines to the situation.

1. Consult with your pediatrician. Certain physical problems can cause depressed feelings. When a child suffers from long-term depression,

Failing to recognize that mistakes and failures can be corrected. ("I'll never get it right.")

Refusing to admit to a mistake or failure in order to save face. ("Why do I always lose?")

Rejecting the need to learn or grow. ("What difference will it make if I know that or not?")

Unwillingness to share with others. ("I rarely get anything worthwhile, so why should I share it? I'm going to keep it all for me.")

Blaming others for difficulties and problems. ("Others try to make my life hard.")

Rejecting spiritual teachings that could help. ("Why would God love *me*? I don't believe it.")[5]

it's important to consult your pediatrician for possible organic causes and treatments.

2. Help your child learn to express depressed feelings. Keep in mind that depression robs people of the ability to govern their thinking and emotions. If your depressed child just stares, ignores greetings, or turns away from you, remember that he doesn't *want* to act that way. He's not trying to punish you. A severely depressed child can't control himself any more than you could walk a straight line after twirling around twenty times.

Your child needs to talk about the problems that depress her, but she may avoid doing so. Why? She may think you're not interested, that her problems will seem insignificant to you. Or it may be difficult for her to bring up the topic. This is when your availability becomes crucial to your child's survival. Spend enough time with your child to allow for informal talks that open the door to more serious discussions. You can use the Ball of Grief or the Five Fingers of Feelings at this time (see chapter 9).

When your child does begin to talk about his or her feelings, follow these important guidelines:

- Understand what is being said from your child's point of view. His interpretation of matters (which might be considerably different from yours) is important since his beliefs will largely determine what he does in the future.
- Be sure your nonverbal expressions indicate a genuine interest in what your child is saying. Avoid anything that might distract you from focusing directly on your child. Lean down to his or her level, or sit on the floor.
- Use gentle, open-ended questions to gather information from your child. Avoid implying wrongdoing or guilt by your tone.

- Withhold giving your opinions, information, or advice until your child is ready for it. Let him or her decide whether you will listen or offer suggestions.
- Control your own emotions. It will help your child maintain composure. A power struggle at this point could intensify your child's feelings.
- Don't try to fill every moment with words. Silence can allow your child to organize his thoughts.
- Watch your child's nonverbal expressions. Look for the feelings that lie beneath your child's words.
- Allow for disagreement. Your child's perspective may be different from yours.[6]

Most of us, as parents, have a difficult time coming up with what to say. It's not an everyday occurrence, so it stretches our ability to say something helpful. Here are some suggestions:

"I am so sorry this happened."

"I'm glad you're okay, even though it was upsetting."

"Remember when you broke a bone? Eventually it healed. Your heart will heal in time as well, but it will probably take longer than you want."

"Sadness is what anyone would feel after something like this."

"You would like to forget this. We all would. But it's too painful to forget right now."

"It's all right to cry."

"Your feelings will change from day to day. Sometimes they're all mixed together."

"Even adults sometimes feel confused about their feelings."

"I'd like to make your pain go away, but I can't."

"Sometimes you forget, and sometimes it comes back again."

"Remember when the dentist put Novocain in your mouth to pull your tooth? It felt numb. After something like this, you feel numb."[7]

Ask your child: "Which of these feelings would you like to talk to God about?" and "How would you like Jesus to help you at this time?" One of the promises of Scripture that can be shared is Isaiah 25:8: "The Lord GOD will wipe tears away from all faces" (NASB).

3. Give support and make adjustments. The whole family needs to be informed and coached when one of its members is depressed. Ask each person to avoid conflicts, put-downs, and unrealistic expectations until things are back to normal. Suspend confrontation and strong discipline until you can restore stability.

4. Don't avoid your depressed child. Avoiding the depressed child further isolates her and worsens the problem. Don't allow yourself to feel guilty and somehow responsible for her depression. Remember that while someone may contribute to another's problems from time to time, no one person is responsible for another's happiness.

5. Realize that your depressed child is a hurting child. Don't tell a depressed child to just snap out of it. Avoid offering simple solutions like "Just pray about it" or "Read your Bible more." And never imply that a child is using depression to solicit sympathy. To a depressed child, emotional pain is as intense as physical pain, if not more so.

6. Empathize rather than sympathize with your child. Do you know the difference? Sympathy only reinforces someone's feelings of hopelessness. Statements such as "It's awful that you're depressed" and "You must feel miserable" tend to encourage helplessness and low self-esteem. Instead, let the child know you've had similar experiences and that you know these feelings will pass. Help is available.

7. Reconstruct your child's self-esteem. One of the most important steps a parent can take is to help rebuild a child's self-esteem, because when depression occurs, self-esteem tends to crumble. A depressed child doesn't understand his value as God's creation. He doesn't *feel* the extent of God's love for him. Because of this, he doubts everyone's love as well.

Because a depressed child is unwilling to participate in normal activity, it won't be easy to involve her in opportunities that reinforce self-worth. It might be better just to get the child involved without a lot of discussion. Involve her in activities you know she enjoys—and in which she has experienced success. Focus her attention on her accomplishments. And don't let your child's apathy discourage you. Remember, your child is cautious right now and lacks enthusiasm for life. In time, her excitement will return.[8]

8. Watch your child's diet. A depressed child may have no appetite, but nutrition is still important. Don't let food become another issue by harping on it or using guilt to get him to eat. Instead, explain to your child that, hungry or not, it's important to nourish the body. Sit with your child and try to make mealtimes an enjoyable family event.

9. Keep your child busy. To the severely depressed child, physical activity is more beneficial than mental activity. So take charge of planning your child's activities. If he's lost interest in things he usually enjoys, remind him of the fun he's had in the past, and then gently but firmly insist that he become involved.

Don't ask him if he wants to do something; he'll probably decline. And don't allow yourself to become frustrated and say something like, "You're going with me because I'm sick and tired of you feeling sorry for yourself." Instead, you might say something like, "I know you haven't been feeling well, but you are entitled to some fun. I think you might like this once we get started. I want to share this activity with you."

Use any activity your child enjoys, and be aware that you may need to schedule his entire day for him. But by getting him involved, you help him begin to break destructive behavior patterns and gain energy and motivation.

10. Never tease or belittle your child for a lack of self-confidence. Neither showcase nor ignore low self-esteem. It is a common problem of depression and must be faced. Don't argue about or participate in your child's self-pity, but present the illogical nature of her self-disparagement. Remind her of past accomplishments, and help her focus on her abilities. If she says, "I can't do anything," gently recount her skills and talents. In time, as her confidence builds, she will begin to overcome her sense of helplessness.

Remember, if your child experiences depression, see it as a message: Something is wrong, and you need to take action to find the cause.

11. Watch out for the possibility of suicide. You may be shocked by this, but children do sometimes take their own lives. The family of any depressed person should be aware of the possibility, and any suspicions of suicide should be taken seriously. Unfortunately, the incidence of suicide is on the rise, and a child or adolescent who expresses utter hopelessness for the future may be at risk. If he is able to talk about his suicidal thoughts or plans, he may be willing to solicit your support and help.

To conclude this chapter, I'd like to leave you with a word from writer Madeleine L'Engle. She seems to speak about how any of us—children or adults—feel when depressed...and how we can remember something important at just those times:

It is when things go wrong, when the good things do not happen, when our prayers seem to have been lost, that God is most present. We do not need the sheltering wings when things go smoothly. We are closest to God in the darkness, stumbling along blindly.[9]

Chapter 12

Divorce:
A Never-Ending Grief

Newsweek magazine has estimated that 45 percent of all children will live with only one parent at some time before they are eighteen years old. Twelve million children under the age of eighteen now have parents who are divorced. By the year 2008, the "traditional family" in our country will be the stepfamily. We're moving to a family structure in which the majority of children could experience divorce. And for many, it's not just once.

Your family may be intact, but your child will have many friends who come from divorced homes. Since they may look to you as a model of an intact family, you may end up ministering to these children. So you need to be aware of the effect of divorce upon their lives.

The authors of *The Unexpected Legacy of Divorce* say:

Divorce is a life-transforming experience. After divorce, childhood is different. Adolescence is different. Adulthood—with the decision to marry or not and have children or not—is different....

From the viewpoint of the children, and counter to what happens to their parents, divorce is a cumulative experience. Its impact increases over time and rises to a crescendo in adulthood. In adulthood it affects personality, the ability to trust, expectations about relationships, and ability to cope with change.

The first upheaval occurs at the breakup. Children are frightened and angry, terrified of being abandoned by both parents, and they feel responsible for the divorce. Most children are taken by surprise; few are relieved.

As the post-divorce family took shape, their world increasingly resembled what they feared most. Home was a lonely place. The household was in disarray for years. Many children were forced to move, leaving behind familiar schools, close friends and other supports.

As the children told us, adolescence begins early in divorced homes and, compared with that of youngsters raised in intact families, is more likely to include more early sexual experiences for girls and higher alcohol and drug use for girls and boys. Adolescence is more prolonged in divorced families and extends well into the years of early adulthood.

But it's in adulthood that children of divorce suffer the most. The impact of divorce hits them most cruelly as they go in search of love, sexual intimacy, and commitment.[1]

What Is Divorce Like for a Child?

A child certainly doesn't want a divorce. He is like a bystander caught in a flood, swept away by the current, having to drift with the flow. And a child caught in a divorce experiences multiple losses. These can include not only the loss of one of the parents but also the loss of a home, neighborhood, school friends, the family standard of living, family outings, family holiday get-togethers, and so on. Other losses might include:

- The loss of the expectation that "my family will be together forever"
- The loss of trust: "If I can't depend on my parents, who can I depend on?"
- The loss of the familiar, the routine, and the safe
- The possible loss of frequent access to a set of grandparents as well as the addition of a new set (with a remarriage)
- The loss of part of their childhood

Were you aware that, in a divorce, children often lose *both* parents? The distress of the breakup, coupled with the daily demands of being a single parent, can make a mother and father less available to their children, physically and emotionally. Both tend to be less emotionally responsive to their children.[2]

And have you ever wondered what it would be like to learn, as a child, that your parents were divorcing and then in this panic to begin telling your friends? Fear becomes a daily companion.

Children experiencing the crisis of divorce frequently must deal with ongoing or repeated experiences of loss coupled with feelings of rejection. In many cases, the decision to divorce is preceded by one or more parental separations involving the departure of one parent from the existing family. The child faces the additional complexity of knowing that the parental decision to separate and divorce was made by choice, which at some level is experienced by the youngster as a rejection. Typically, the youngster is also expected to develop relationships with subsequent parent substitutes and newly acquired siblings.[3]

When there is the loss of a parent, there also may be a loss of hope for the future. An uncertainty worms its way into the child's mind; she can feel out of control to a greater extent than ever before. The stable parents upon whom she depended are no longer that solid rock. This may occur in a practical area such as finances. If a divorced father has promised to take care of the family through his monthly payments, what must a child feel when payments become irregular and eventually cease?

Divorce affects children in different ways, depending on the age of the child. Let's look closer.

Ages three to six. Young children experience deeper fears, and the routine separations of life become traumatic. A parent's going shopping or the child's leaving for school is now a stressful experience. Children tend to regress to earlier behavior and become more passive and dependent. More and more they ask "what's that?" questions, which is their effort to overcome the disorganization of crisis.

Many in this age group will regress. They may refuse to feed themselves, and some even revert to a need for diapers. The child can create wild and imaginative fantasies in his mind, because he is puzzled by what's happening to him. He's bewildered. Play doesn't have the same sense of fun.

Throughout all the stages of childhood, a common line of thinking abounds: *Did I cause my parents' divorce? Am I responsible for not having a family anymore?* These preschoolers may become aggressive with other children. Boys tend to become noisier, angrier, more restless, and more disruptive in group activities. Some girls become angry, but many become little adults, trying to be perfect and acting like a parent.[4]

Ages six to eight. A child in this age group has his own set of reactions. Sadness is there, but his sense of responsibility for the parents' breakup becomes stronger. He has deep feelings of loss. He is afraid of being abandoned and sometimes even of starving. He yearns for the parent who has left. Many are convinced their parent has rejected them.

Separation anxieties begin to emerge. A four-year-old who looked forward to her nursery school playground before the divorce now clings to her mother and cries, refusing to leave. Her six-year-old brother used to go to bed at night happily. Now he avoids bedtime, making one request after another. It's water, bathroom, or...protection from monsters. Actually, he wants to see his mother. Baby-sitters don't like to come to this home anymore. Too many temper tantrums!

Frequently these children are angry with the parent who cares for them all the time. They have conflicting loyalties. They want to love both parents but struggle with the feeling that loving one is being disloyal to the other. Thus they feel torn and confused. Symptoms can include nail-biting, bedwetting, loss of sleep, and retreating into fantasy to solve family problems. Children of both age groups become possessive.

Ages eight to twelve. Preadolescent children usually experience anger as their main emotional response. This anger is directed toward the parent they feel is responsible for the family breakup, and this could be the custodial parent. They're prone to take sides. But anger, instead of coming out directly at the parent, may be directed at peers. Thus these kids may alienate potential friends at the time when they most need them. Their self-image is shaken. Sometimes they throw themselves with great intensity into what they are doing, such as play or projects, as their way of handling the disruption of their lives. For about half of the children in this group, school performance drops markedly.

This is a time of conscience development, and the divorce may have a shattering effect upon that process. Watch closely for psychosomatic illnesses at this stage.

The child's reaction at any age will vary and often depends upon the behavior and reaction of the two parents. When parents fight hatefully, battle over child custody, and use the child to get back at each other, expect emotional turmoil in the child. Children don't have the emotional resources to cope with this amount of stress.

Some parents actually use bribery in an effort to win the allegiance of a child. Sadly, some children learn to manipulate both parents and pit one against the other. The more emotional turmoil involved in a divorce, the more potential harm to a child.[5]

In all the turmoil, the child seems to have two major concerns. First, she dreams of her parents reconciling. If this were to happen, all her problems would end. She believes, in spite of previous problems, that the family was better off when both parents were there. She may have witnessed all the conflict, but she's usually willing to endure it to have an intact family. After all, this is the only family she knows.

Her second concern revolves around herself: *What's going to happen to me?* She's afraid the custodial parent will abandon her. One parent has already left her, so why shouldn't the other eventually do the same? If one parent was forced to leave, as many are, the child's fear centers on being thrown out, just as his mother or father was. Another fear concerns being replaced in his parents' affection by someone else. As the custodial parent begins to date, the child wonders if this new person is going to become important to his parent. And if so, she fears she may lose the time and attention she now receives.

REQUIRED: PASSING THROUGH THE EMOTIONAL STAGES

Whether a child's home is quiet and peaceful or filled with visible conflict, the child rarely expects a divorce. He may not like the conflict but hopes it will settle down eventually. Discovering the impending divorce shocks the child's system. All the mixed feelings come crashing in.

The child passes through some fairly well-defined emotional stages as he struggles to understand and deal with the divorce. These stages are normal, and they cannot be avoided or bypassed. *A child needs to pass through these stages in order to produce positive growth and minimize the negative effects.*

Stage #1: Fear and anxiety. The child stares into the mist of an unknown future. A home and family with two parents was once the child's source of stability. That family now shatters.

So what do the fear and anxiety look like? You'll observe restlessness, nightmares, sleeplessness, stomach problems, sweating, and all kinds of aches and pains. These are normal reactions. Parents at this time need to offer reassurance and discuss their plans in detail. It is important to give facts, because a child's imagination may run wild. *Knowing* is better than *wondering.* A child may tend to think up worse problems than actually exist.

Stage #2: Abandonment and rejection. After fear and anxiety come feelings of abandonment and rejection. The feelings of the initial stage recede and are replaced by this new struggle. The child may know at one level that he will not be rejected or abandoned, but he is still concerned that it might happen. A younger child finds it hard to distinguish between the parents' leaving one another and their leaving *him.* And he may focus on this. This stage may be perpetuated by unkept promises on the part of the parent who leaves.

Stage #3: Aloneness and sadness. These soon replace abandonment and rejection. As the family structure changes and settles down, the reality of what has occurred begins to settle in. A child feels this stage with a pain in the stomach and a tightness in the chest. This is a time for depression, and regular activities tend to be neglected. Many children do a lot of thinking, which is usually wishful daydreaming. And the fantasies follow the same theme—parents getting together again and everything being all right. Crying spells may become more frequent at this time.

Stage #4: Frustration and anger. Children whose parents divorce or separate are angry children. This is a natural response to the frustration they feel. In addition, they have seen angry and upset parents; the child begins to emulate this modeled behavior. Anger may continue to be the pattern for many years and may carry over into many relationships.

The anger may not show itself directly though. It may be suppressed or masked. It may come out through negativity and moodiness. Whether expressed or not, it can be damaging. If it is there, it is far better for it to be admitted and handled rather than buried and waiting for an eventual explosion.

The child's anger is there for several reasons. It serves as a protection and a warning signal, just like depression. It is alerting the person to a problem and is often a reaction to hurt, fear, or frustration. It's an involuntary response, and parents and counselors alike shouldn't be threatened by it or attempt to deny its presence in the child. If it is not allowed a direct expression, it will exhibit itself in a passive and indirect manner, which is far more dangerous. If it is stuffed and turned inward, it will harden into depression.

So be on the lookout for the signs of indirect expression. Sarcasm and resistance are fairly easy to spot, but other manifestations may occur in physical complaints such as asthma, vomiting, insomnia, and stomachaches. The child's anger may be expressed through a negative perspective on life, irritability, withdrawal, self-isolation, and resistance to school chores—or whatever the child wants to resist.

It's essential to accept the normalcy of the child's anger, no matter how it's displayed. Encourage the child to talk it out but not to act it out in uncontrolled rage.

The feeling of anger should never be denied. Rather, help your child learn to express and drain it. Cognitively, he can talk, talk, talk it through. But he also needs permission to let his body display what's happening inside. As he speaks, let him know he can furrow his brow, grit his teeth, or raise his voice. That is how an angry person looks and acts, after all. It is appropriate. He can be given a punching bag to hit, a rubber ball to squeeze, or a towel to twist. Let him know that this is a controlled way of showing one's appropriate emotions. In designated areas of your house, he might be given his special places to cry and scream out his pain. According to his ability, help him understand the *reason* for his anger, its *purpose,* and its *means* of controlled release.

Stage #5: Rejection and resentment. Eventually the child's anger moves into rejection and resentment. The child is not over his angry feelings but is now attempting to create some emotional distance between himself and his parent. This is a protective device. Pouting can be one form of rejection, as can "the silent treatment." The child won't respond to suggestions or commands and often "forgets" to follow through with what he's supposed to do. He becomes hypercritical.[6]

This behavior is actually what psychologists call *reaction formation.* Paradoxically, as a child pushes a parent away, he really wants to be close to the parent. He shouts hateful statements and yet wants to be loving. He is just trying to protect himself from rejection, so he rejects others first.

Stage #6: Reestablishment of trust. The final stage in the process of dealing with divorce is the reestablishment of trust. It is difficult to say how long this will take, as it varies with each situation and child and can range from months to years.

If you're concerned about the effects of divorce on your child, you can do the following:

- Do not be overly concerned with your own feelings to the neglect of the child's feelings. Each day give him some time to discuss what he is experiencing and feeling.
- Give the child time to process her feelings. There are no quick solutions or cures.
- Determine to continue living in the same home and neighborhood, keeping things the same as much as possible. A stable environment benefits your child. The greater the change, the greater the stress and discomfort in him.
- Offer opportunities to accomplish tasks and to demonstrate responsibility. Then give positive feedback about her successes. This is what builds a child's sense of self-confidence and self-esteem.
- Reassure him that he is not the cause of the divorce or separation. Both parents need to give consistent and equal amounts of love.
- According to the child's level of understanding, help her to know in advance the different types of feelings she will experience. Keep the child informed at all times of any expected changes so she can prepare.

Convey the assurance that even though Mom and Dad will be working through their own struggles, *both* of them will be taking care of him. In addition, guide a child in selecting some task he can accomplish. This will help him overcome a feeling of helplessness. And finally, make sure your child knows that, though parents are imperfect, he has a heavenly Parent who will never fail him—the One who is always there for him:

And surely I am with you always, to the very end of the age....

Because God has said, "Never will I leave you; never will I forsake you." (Matthew 28:20; Hebrews 13:5)

Chapter 13

Trauma: It Shouldn't Happen to a Child

We used to say that in the United States few children experience human-perpetrated disasters. Oklahoma City began a great change. Then came the World Trade Center and Pentagon disasters of September 11, 2001. The repeated viewing of these cataclysmic events, especially the planes ramming into the towers and those shiny skyscrapers cascading down in a smoky mass of destruction and death, have virtually tattooed these images on the minds of our children. At the time, *USA Today* told of preschool kids building towers out of LEGOs and then crashing toy planes into them again and again saying, "They're dead. All the people are dead."

These are the traumatic events that draw national attention. But trauma of any kind turns the life of a child upside down. Some children experience it *directly.* It happens through accidents at school, in the attacks on our crime-ridden streets, or in the midst of secret, everyday violence at home. Other children experience trauma *vicariously.* That is, with the media's constant replaying of mayhem and chaos, our wide-eyed children take on a new identity that is now described by a newly coined term just for them: "livingroom witnesses."

It is not a harmless phenomenon. To children, a trauma is a wound, an ongoing, festering sore that strikes frightening messages into their souls:

Your world is no longer safe.

Your world is no longer kind.

Your world is no longer predictable.

Your world is no longer trustworthy.

It's difficult enough for adults to handle this. But children don't have an adult's mental or verbal ability or the life experiences to draw upon as they attempt to cope and find comfort. A child's mind doesn't work the same way as ours. It's less sophisticated and processes information differently. The trauma brings into their lives a silence, an isolation, a feeling of helplessness. And there are warning signs that a child isn't doing well.

- He consistently doesn't want to go to school; grades drop and don't recover.
- He loses all interest or pleasure in what he used to enjoy.
- He talks about hurting or killing himself.
- He hears or sees things others don't.
- He can't eat or sleep enough to remain healthy.[1]

Trauma is a condition characterized by the phrase "I just can't seem to get over it." And it's not just for those who've been through a war. I've observed it in a father who saw his daughter fatally crushed in an accident and in women who were sexually abused as children or who experienced an abortion. I've seen it in the paramedic, the chaplain, the nurse, the survivor of a robbery or traffic accident or rape, and in those subjected to intense pressure or harassment in the workplace. And I saw it on the faces of those in New York on 9/11.

The saddest thing is to see it in a child. All of us parents pray it won't happen in our family.

KNOW THESE THREE *B*s OF TRAUMA

We pray to be spared because we know that trauma is much worse than a crisis. Trauma is the response to any event that shatters your safe world so that it's no longer a place of refuge. And we instinctively know that children need safety more than adults do.

Yes, trauma is more than a state of crisis. It is a normal reaction to abnormal events that overwhelm a person's ability to adapt to life. Trauma makes you feel powerless. It's overwhelming for adults and life-shattering for children. If you had the ability to scan little Timmy when he's experienced a trauma, what would you see?

What's happening in his BRAIN. Timmy's thinking process has been distorted. He will experience confusion, a distortion of time, difficulties in solving problems and in figuring out what's best to do next.

In other words, as a result of trauma, something happens in the brain that affects the way Timmy processes information. It affects how he (or any person, for that matter) interprets and stores the event he's experienced. In effect, it overrides his alarm system.

This will make more sense as you think of young children in their preschool years. Are they mature in any way? Not really. And especially their brains are immature. At a time of trauma the child's brain tissue and chemistry are actually changed by sensitization. The child's brain is malleable, and it begins to organize itself around the experience of the trauma.

Hypersensitivity can actually become wired into basic brain chemistry and bodily functions. Not only that, after a trauma occurs, some of the attention and capacities in the brain, which were originally set aside for learning other skills, may be pushed aside from their original purposes to help defend against future traumas. In subtle ways the child's brain goes on alert. It's in a "prevent trauma" mode. And after enough chronic experiences, this arousal state becomes a "trait." The child's brain organizes around the overactivated systems to make sure the child survives. Other skills are sacrificed by their defensive posture. It's not a pleasant way to live.[2]

What's happening in his BODY. Timmy's body is out of sync. His heart is probably pounding. He's got nausea, cramps, sweating, headaches, and even muffled hearing. Emotionally, he's riding a roller coaster. He's irritable, afraid, anxious, frustrated, and angry.

Since Timmy's alarm system is stuck, he's hyperaroused. He could suffer from high blood pressure, rapid heart rate or irregular beat, slightly elevated temperature, and constant anxiety. He may go through his life with his alarm button on alert, constantly on the watch for any possible threat.

What's happening in his BEHAVIOR. The bottom line is that if Timmy has experienced a trauma, whether an accident, death, divorce, abuse, or whatever it might be, his parents ought to expect extremes of behavior—either overresponding or underresponding.

Either way, Timmy's behavior is off. He's probably slower in what he does, wanders aimlessly, is dejected, has difficulty remembering, and could be hysterical, out of control, and hyper.[3]

What Are Some Age-Characteristic Responses?

With physical trauma, obviously some part of the body is impacted with such a powerful force that the body's natural protection, such as skin or bones, can't prevent the injury, and the body's normal, natural healing capabilities can't mend the injury without some assistance.

Perhaps not as obvious is the emotional wounding of trauma. A child's emotions can be so assaulted that his belief about life, his will to grow, his spirit, his dignity, and his sense of security are significantly damaged. He ends up feeling helpless. An adult can experience this to some degree in a crisis and still bounce back. In trauma, even an adult has difficulty bouncing back because he'll experience derealization ("Is this really happening?") and depersonalization ("I don't know what I really stand for anymore"). So trauma is indescribable, even for adults.

But you're reading this book out of concern for your child. So, as I've done in previous chapters, I'd like to break down the childhood responses and reactions by age groups. This is because children of different ages are in different stages of cognitive and emotional development when they're traumatized. The very nature of brain development causes them to respond in age-related ways. Therefore we need to know what to expect at certain ages. The following are characteristics of children who have experienced trauma. These posttraumatic stress disorder symptoms are unique to children.

Children under four years old. They tend to "forget" their trauma experiences (consciously, at least for a period of time), although a few may remember from the beginning. Those over this age do remember and tend to remember the experiences vividly, whereas adults often tend to deny reality or repress their memories. Briefly, here are the prominent characteristics:

1. Most of these kids don't experience the psychic numbing common to adults. But if it's parental abuse, they do.

2. Most don't experience intrusive and disruptive visual flashbacks.

3. School performance usually isn't impacted in acute trauma for as long a time as adults' work performance is impacted.

4. Play and reenactment increases in frequency. And with a child you will find frequent time distortions.[4]

Children of preschool or kindergarten age. Here are the most likely posttraumatic behaviors you'll observe:

1. Withdrawal. This is common, since children react to a trauma with a generalized response of distrust. Because of their limited thinking and processing ability, they can't feel safe from experiencing hurt again. They may be struggling to make sense of what they've just learned (which is overwhelmingly negative) about the world. And they may be totally silent around others, as though they're living in their own world.

2. Denial. This to be expected, including denial of the facts and of memories of the event. They may avoid certain issues or ignore certain people. Distortions are common. Some children embellish the truth or develop gaps in what they remember.

3. Anxious attachments. These can include clinging, whining, not letting go of parents or favorite possessions, and throwing tantrums more frequently. Attachment adjustments during this stage are somewhat common.

4. Fears. These could include being afraid of new situations, specific objects, strangers, males, or being restricted or confined. Such fears could occur at home, on the playground, or in the classroom. A child may balk at talking about a specific subject or won't read a certain story or might refuse to go to a certain place or room. Some are reluctant to go home.

If there are problems with sleeping, then fear may be the cause (the best way to avoid repetitive nightmares is to stay awake). A child may wake up frequently at night. He may be dreaming about what happened. In order to find some comfort in his life, he will likely regress to behavior that worked in earlier developmental stages.

Younger school-age children. Everything mentioned about preschool children could emerge during this stage as well. But there are some additional posttraumatic characteristics.

1. Performance decline. Things go downhill in schoolwork, sports, hobbies, music. If this occurs, it could be because the child is acting out or because he is preoccupied with what transpired in his life.

2. Compensatory behavior. Your child begins trying to compensate for the event itself or the results. There's a purpose to this response, whether he is aware of it or not. It's his attempt to deny what occurred, to reverse it, or to gain some control or retribution. This could occur through fantasy, playing the event out with others (with a different ending), or talking it out with others.

3. Obsessive talking. You may end up with what some parents call a chatterbox. Your child talks nonstop. As one mother said, "He wouldn't talk about it for some time, but once he started, it was all the time, over and over again. I can't turn him off. It seems to accelerate once he starts. When he writes something for class, he always weaves in the incident."

4. Inappropriate expressions. This is a common response, even with adults, since in trauma there is a separation or disconnection of the functioning of the left and right sides of the brain. Sometimes a person experiences a flood of feelings (the right side of the brain), but she has no narrative from the left side to explain those feelings. Or the actual events and story may be quite vivid...but there's no emotion at this time.

5. Repetitive reenactments. A child of this age plays differently from your preschooler. So expect more reenactments of the event in his play and great detail. They don't necessarily help the child in his recovery, but it's another means of expression.

What do children do when they play a compensatory or reenactment game? They may kill the perpetrator, and if you walk in on this scenario, don't put a stop to it. It's purposeful. Their play may involve acting as if life were normal, as it used to be. Or their play theme may revolve around undoing the damage.

I would expect your child to exhibit such changes in behavior. These are outward signs of inner confusion. A calm, steady child may become impulsive and bounce from one thing to another. He could regress. Just remember there is a purpose to what your child is doing. He's trying, in the best way he knows how, to relieve his tension and anxiety. He's trying to get attention so he can build back his sense of security. Or, since his view of life and the world has been turned upside down, he's just trying to sort through all the wreckage.

All of the changes in behavior and reenactment are stress reducers. If the stress isn't reduced, his body will begin to keep score. Physical complaints will increase, and these are symptoms of his distress. Heading the list are stomachaches, headaches, and digestive upsets. On occasion your child may use these symptoms to get attention or to avoid further stress.

Older children and adolescents. Adolescents, and those on the verge of this stage, tend to act out their distress when they have experienced a trauma. Often their acting out is purposeless and destructive. They're less apt to turn to you as a parent for help; instead, they'll turn to their peers. In addition, you may encounter the following:

1. Self-isolation. Often we see a teen isolating himself, using drugs or alcohol, sexually acting out, cutting school or church, running away, and getting involved in suicidal activity. Sometimes the trauma isn't recent but occurred at a young age. Yet his ability to block the event has now diminished because of the changes of adolescence. This stage of development, in and of itself, is a crisis.

2. Decreased self-esteem. This will be coupled with an increase in self-criticism. After all, adolescents believe they're able to control their life at this stage, and when they can't, it's devastating to them. Self-blame is one of their first choices.

3. Acting adultlike. Sometimes a traumatized adolescent develops an older lifestyle too rapidly. These teens are described as "too old, too fast!" They take on adult responsibilities prematurely, and there's very little joy in their life.

4. Displaced anger. This is the kind of anger that misses the legitimate target. Instead, innocent adults and parents usually take the hit.[5]

How can you as a parent help at a time of trauma—during and after? Children and adolescents themselves have identified what they need as well as what they *don't* need in a trauma or crisis. Here is what they've said worked:

My mom or dad
> ...allowed me to talk.
> ...showed warmth and acceptance.
> ...listened well.
> ...respected my privacy.
> ...showed patience.
> ...showed understanding.
> ...made helpful suggestions.
> ...was there when I needed her/him.

Adolescents also identified three types of adult responses that seem to make things worse. One style is the *withholding parent,* in which parents tend to focus on their own needs rather than the child's. They also deny the seriousness of the child's or adolescent's experiences and discount their feelings. This could alienate your child. *Incompetent parents* glibly give false reassurance, discourage discussion about the problem, and have difficulty themselves handling what happened or fulfilling their role as parents at this time. A third type is the *reactive/escapist parent* who makes false assumptions about the child's role in the incident, which usually leads to blaming the child. With this parent, the teen shuts down and stops talking about it. These three styles, if reflected during a child's crisis, lead to adolescent problems.[6]

Some Definite DON'Ts

When helping your child or adolescent, you would be wise to *avoid* these types of interaction after a trauma:

DON'T fall apart. Even though you are upset, stay together for your children. Falling apart tells a child or adolescent that you can't really be trusted with what they have shared with you. It's essential for you to stay in emotional control. If you know it's going to be a difficult day or you're beginning to get shaky, hand off your responsibilities to someone else. Remember, you are to take care of your children. They probably aren't coping well, and they can't take care of you. Empathy must be in balance.

DON'T speculate. Avoid sharing what you're not sure of or what isn't true. Just say, "I'm not sure, but I'll find out for you." It's a matter of trust. Don't say, "Everything will be all right" unless you are 100 percent sure you know what that means and that it really will be all right. False promises cripple your credibility.

DON'T judge. Avoid any kind of judgments at this point, whether verbal or nonverbal. Focus on the needs of your child rather than what you think "*ought* to be or *should* have been."

DON'T interrogate. You're not an inquisitor. Constant questioning can overwhelm and push your child or adolescent into silence. When questioning, be gentle and give her time to reflect on what you've asked.

DON'T clam up. Even if you don't know what to do or say, don't withdraw. Children and adolescents need you around to support, normalize, and affirm.[7]

DON'T overreact to anger. If children have experienced trauma, their anger may turn into rage or aggression. And these feelings can be confusing and frightening to everyone. It's hard for children to lose trust in people as well as losing the order and security of life. This deep fear spawns intense frustration.

DON'T withdraw support. If children see others happily going on with their lives while their own life is in shambles, resentment builds, and some of the people in their lives may respond as if nothing happened to them. Their experience and pain need to be acknowledged. Most individuals who have experienced a loss also experience a second loss: when the cards and support stop coming. When this happens, they can't help but wonder if others have stopped caring, since the pain continues after the support stops.[8]

SOME DEFINITE DOs

Here's the flip side of the coin. You can respond in positive ways and offer practical help when your child needs it most.

DO encourage emotion. Some of your child's angry expressions may not be acceptable, of course (you can't let him break all the windows in your house or burn down the back porch). But it's important not to overreact and cause your child to begin stifling his feelings. Here are some suggestions. A child can...

- talk it out
- write it out
- act it out in a pantomime
- sing it out
- draw it
- whisper it
- count to 57 in sets of 3 and 4 (for example, 3, 7, 10, 14, 17—this takes some thought!)
- use exercise: running in place, hopping on one foot, hitting a tetherball, etc.

If your child is shouting his anger at you, tell him you want to hear him, but it's easier for you to hear when he talks slower. Give him some guidelines:

- It's all right to feel angry.
- It's *not* all right to hit others.
- The goal is *controlled* release of anger.
- Ask: "Where is the anger in your body?"
- Ask: "What does anger look like on your face?"

DO normalize the reactions. Keep in mind that a trauma can change a child's life forever. It's as though she gets on a roller coaster, but this one never stops. It's like having a nightmare when you're not asleep. And the experience changes from day to day. One day the event comes back in vivid color, the next day it's black and white, and the next day she doesn't remember it, and the next day she's numb. This all comes packaged with the fears "I'll never be the same again," "What if it happens again?" and "I'll be left all alone."

The best approach you can take is to love, comfort, and offer reassurance that you're there for your child. You *normalize* her reactions and feelings. Here's how you might say it:

> "I'm wondering if all your feelings are kind of confusing. That's normal. You're not going crazy. What *happened* was crazy."

> "You know, you're going to feel off balance for a while. It's like trying to stand on one foot. That's all right. It may help you feel better."

> "There's nothing wrong or weird or bad about your feeling this way. Any person—child or adult—would feel the same after something like this. It will be helpful to tell me what you need and how I can help."

> "Sometimes it's hard to talk about feelings. We'll work together and find some easier ways to let them out."[9]

DO encourage. What do children need most in a posttrauma situation? Many of them need to be encouraged just to be patient with themselves. And most of all, they need to know it's all right to feel and express feelings.

DO return to childhood. Attempt to return traumatized children to the world of childhood as soon as possible. They need the routine of school, recreation, bedtime, sports, church, clubs, parties, etc. A child responds better when he regains the environment that gives him back the security of the routine. A child needs to be given the permission to be a child again.[10]

If you don't see progress, don't hesitate. Take your child to a skilled therapist who understands children's trauma. There is hope.

Remembering Grandparents

One of the most common losses for a child is the loss of a grandparent, and aside from the loss of a pet, it's often the first. This person is the link to your child's past. Grandparents fill a child's life with memories of the child's own parents in a unique way. They often describe a world that is totally foreign to the child's world.

Children know their grandparents won't always be with them. So when a grandparent begins to fail physically or mentally, don't be afraid to talk with your child about this. Talk about your own feelings and your own grief concerning your parents.

One author suggests using a "remembering page" to help children commemorate the life of a grandparent. Here's an example:[1]

———◆———

A Kid's Remembering Page

This is a story about (grandparent's name).

My grandparent was born on (date).

Her (his) parents' names were _____, and she (he) grew up in (town/state/country). She (he) had _____ sisters and _____

brothers. She (he) married _____, my grandfather
(grandmother), and lived in (town/state/country).

My mother (father) was one of ___ children.

My grandparent loved to _____.

She (he) didn't like _____.

When I visited her (him), I really liked to _____.

My favorite thing that my grandparent gave me is _____.

What I will miss most about my grandparent is _____.

If I am a grandparent someday, I would like to _____.

On the back of this page, I have drawn a picture of my grandparent and me (doing)…

Helping Children Tell Their Traumatic Story

Debra Whiting Alexander, author of *Children Changed by Trauma*, offers verbal prompts that parents can use to draw children out in conversation. She says:

> When there's been a crisis or trauma it's important to help children feel free to speak their minds and to voluntarily tell you about their experiences of what happened. Never force or pressure them to tell you anything they are not yet willing to verbalize. Once they feel safe and comfortable, they may want to share with you what they went through. Here is a list of what you can say to support children who are ready to tell you their story.
>
> If you as the parent have also experienced this same event someone else may be needed to talk with your child as well as you. But someone needs to talk in this manner:
>
> - It's often helpful to talk about what happened.
> - Talking about what happened can help you let go of painful thoughts and memories.

- Draw a picture of what's in your mind. Write a story about what's in your mind.
- Thoughts cannot make bad things happen or prevent them from happening.
- I can handle whatever you would like to tell me about. Your thoughts don't scare or worry me.
- Anything you think about is normal for what you have been through.
- How do you imagine you might think about this in the future? in one week; three months; five years; when you're a grown up?
- Having frightening thoughts does not mean you are going crazy. What happened was crazy, you are not.
- The trauma is over. You have survived the pain it caused, and with time you will survive the memory, too.
- It's important to talk about what you're going through and what you've been through when you are ready.
- What is your understanding of what happened?
- What do you know about it?
- What do you want to know?
- What do you wonder about it?
- Where were you when it happened?
- What were you doing?
- How did you hear about it?
- Who was involved? Who else was there?
- What did you think about when it happened?
- What did you say to yourself?
- What do you remember seeing, hearing, smelling, touching and/or tasting?

- What most concerned you?
- What's your most painful moment or memory?
- What was your first reaction?
- What's not being talked about?
- Are other people right or wrong about what they're saying happened?
- What was handled well?
- Who was helpful and why?
- All of your thoughts before, during and after the event are normal.[1]

Helpful Resources

1. For multiple resources, contact the Dougy Center. The mission of the Dougy Center is to provide loving support in a safe place where children, teens, and their families who are grieving a death can share their experiences as they move through their healing process. Through the National Center for Grieving Children and Families, support and training locally, nationally, and internationally are provided to individuals and organizations seeking to assist children and teens in grief.

The Dougy Center serves children and teens, ages three through nineteen, who have experienced the death of a parent or sibling (or, in the teen groups, a friend) to accident, illness, suicide, or murder. The support groups are coordinated by professional staff members and trained volunteers. In addition, the parents (or caregivers) of the youth participate in support groups to address their needs and the issues of raising children following a traumatic loss.

The Dougy Center
3909 SE 52nd Ave.
PO Box 86852
Portland, OR 97286

Phone: (503) 775-5683

Web site: http://www.dougy.org

2. Consider these additional titles:

Poinsett, Brenda. *Why Do I Feel This Way? What Every Woman Needs to Know About Depression.* Colorado Springs: NavPress, 1996.

Wright, H. Norman. *Winning over Your Emotions.* Eugene, Oreg.: Harvest House, 1998.

Wright, H. Norman and Gary Oliver. *Fears, Doubts, Blues and Pouts.* Colorado Springs: Chariot Victor, 1999. Written for the three- to nine-year-old child, this book covers the emotions of fear, worry, anger, and sadness in story form with extensive discussion questions based upon each child's learning style. Available through Christian Marriage Enrichment at (800) 875-7560.

Notes

Introduction: When Loss Comes Calling

1. Alan D. Wolfelt, *Healing the Bereaved Child: Grief Gardening, Growth Through Grief, and Other Touchstones for Caregivers* (Fort Collins, Colo.: Compassion Press, 1996), 8, adapted.

2. J. William Worden, *Grief Counseling and Grief Therapy: A Handbook for the Mental Health Practitioner* (New York: Springer Publishing, 1982), 10-17.

3. Joy Johnson, *Keys to Helping Children Deal with Death and Grief* (Hauppauge, N.Y.: Barron's Educational Series, 1999), 51-2, adapted.

4. Carol Staudacher, *Beyond Grief: A Guide for Recovering from the Death of a Loved One* (Oakland, Calif.: New Harbinger, 1987), 131-8.

Chapter 1: Looking Loss in the Eye

1. J. William Worden, *Children and Grief: When a Parent Dies* (New York: Guilford Press, 1996), 134, adapted.

2. Martha Wakenshaw, *Caring for Your Grieving Child* (Oakland, Calif.: New Harbinger, 2002), 80-1.

Chapter 2: Face the Hurt or Try to Protect?

1. John W. James and Russell Friedman with Leslie Landon Matthews, *When Children Grieve: For Adults to Help Children Deal with Death, Divorce, Pet Loss, Moving, and Other Losses* (New York: HarperCollins, 2001), 9.

2. James and Friedman, *When Children Grieve*, 17-8, adapted.

3. Claudia Jewett Jarrett, *Helping Children Cope with Separation and Loss* (Boston: Harvard Common Press, 1982), 2-3, adapted.

4. Jarrett, *Helping Children Cope*, 14-5.

5. Kendall Johnson, *Trauma in the Lives of Children: Crisis and Stress Management Techniques for Teachers, Counselors, and Student Service Professionals* (Claremont, Calif.: Hunter House, 1988), 183, adapted.

6. John M. Gottman with Joan DeClaire, *The Heart of Parenting: How to Raise an Emotionally Intelligent Child* (New York: Simon & Schuster, 1997), 52, adapted.

7. Gottman, *The Heart of Parenting*, 73-4.

Chapter 3: Don't Overlook These Two!

1. Lorri A. Greene and Jacquelyn Landis, *Saying Good-bye to the Pet You Love: A Complete Resource to Help You Heal* (Oakland, Calif.: New Harbinger, 2002), 112-21, adapted.

Chapter 4: Sickness...and All Its Big Questions

1. Phyllis Rolfe Silverman, *Never Too Young to Know: Death in Children's Lives* (New York: Oxford University Press, 2000), 115.

2. Joanne M. Hilden and Daniel R. Tobin with Karen Lindsey, *Shelter from the Storm: Caring for a Child with a Life-Threatening Condition* (Cambridge, Mass.: Perseus, 2003), adapted. See introduction and chapters 1-3.

3. Hilden and Tobin, *Shelter from the Storm*, 73-4, adapted.

4. Elisabeth Kübler-Ross, *On Children and Death* (New York: Macmillan, 1983), 68, adapted.

5. Barbara Coloroso, *Parenting Through Crisis: Helping Kids in Times of Loss, Grief and Change* (New York: HarperCollins, 2000), 64-95, adapted.

Chapter 5: In the Family "Machine"—Each Part Affected!

1. Charlotte E. Thompson, *Raising a Handicapped Child: A Helpful Guide for Parents of the Physically Disabled* (New York: Morrow, 1986), 66, adapted.

2. Thomas M. Skric et al., "Severely Handicapped Children and Their Brothers and Sisters," in *Severely Handicapped Young Children and Their Families,* ed. Jan Blacher (Orlando: Academic Press, 1984), 215-46. Discussed in Rosemarie S. Cook, *Parenting a Child with Special Needs* (Grand Rapids, Mich.: Zondervan, 1992), 94-5.

3. Elisabeth Kübler-Ross, *On Children and Death* (New York: Macmillan, 1983), 67-70, adapted.

4. Thompson, *Raising a Handicapped Child,* 62-4.

5. Therese A. Rando, *Grieving: How to Go On Living When Someone You Love Dies* (Lexington, Mass.: Lexington Books, 1988), 178-9, adapted.

6. Lynne Ann DeSpelder and Albert Lee Strickland, *The Last Dance: Encountering Death and Dying* (Mountain View, Calif.: Mayfield Publishing, 1992), 282-3, adapted.

7. Therese A. Rando, ed., *Parental Loss of a Child* (Champaign, Ill.: Research Press, 1986), 323, adapted.

8. Rando, *Parental Loss,* 323-32, adapted.

Chapter 6: The Grieving Family: Roles, Rules, and Responses

1. Joseph Biuso and Brian Newman with Gary Wilde, *Receiving Love* (Wheaton, Ill.: Victor Books, 1996), 44.

2. Biuso and Newman, *Receiving Love,* 178.

3. Mary Ann Emswiler and James P. Emswiler, *Guiding Your Child Through Grief* (New York: Bantam Books, 2000), 47-68.

4. Therese A. Rando, *Grieving: How to Go on Living When Someone You Love Dies* (Lexington, Mass.: Lexington Books, 1988), 121-5, adapted.

5. Viktor E. Frankl, *Man's Search for Meaning* (New York: Simon & Schuster, 1984), 86-7.

6. C. S. Lewis, *Mere Christianity* (New York: Macmillan, 1952), 190.

Chapter 7: It's Different for Them: A Look at Age Differences

1. Dan Schaefer and Christine Lyons, *How Do We Tell the Children? A Parents' Guide to Helping Children Understand and Cope When Someone Dies* (New York: Newmarket Press, 1986), 129, adapted.

2. Maria Trozzi with Kathy Massimini, *Talking with Children About Loss: Words, Strategies, and Wisdom to Help Children Cope with Death, Divorce, and Other Difficult Times* (New York: Perigee, 1999), 18-27, adapted.

3. Carol Staudacher, *Beyond Grief: A Guide for Recovering from the Death of a Loved One* (Oakland, Calif.: New Harbinger, 1987), 129-30, adapted.

4. James A. Fogarty, *The Magical Thoughts of Grieving Children: Treating Children with Complicated Mourning and Advice for Parents* (Amityville, N.Y.: Baywood, 2000), 50.

5. Fogarty, *Magical Thoughts,* 51.

6. William Van Ornum and John B. Mordock, *Crisis Counseling with Children and Adolescents: A Guide for Nonprofessional Counselors* (New York: Continuum, 1983), 21-33.

7. Schaefer and Lyons, *How Do We Tell the Children?* 122.

8. Phyllis Rolfe Silverman, *Never Too Young to Know: Death in Children's Lives* (New York: Oxford University Press, 2000), 53-5, adapted.

9. Therese A. Rando, *Grieving: How to Go on Living When Someone You Love Dies* (Lexington, Mass.: Lexington Books, 1988), 200-4, adapted.

10. Mary Ann Emswiler and James P. Emswiler, *Guiding Your Child Through Grief* (New York: Bantam Books, 2000), 100-6, adapted.

Chapter 8: Think Their Thoughts

1. Sandor B. Brent, "Puns, Metaphors and Misunderstandings in a Two-Year-Old's Conceptions of Death," *Omega Journal of Death and Dying* 8 (1977-78): 285-93, adapted.

2. Lynne Ann DeSpelder and Albert Lee Strickland, *The Last Dance: Encountering Death and Dying* (Mountain View, Calif.: Mayfield Publishing, 1992), 120-3, adapted.

3. Dan Schaefer, as quoted in Joy Johnson, *Keys to Helping Children Deal with Death and Grief* (Hauppauge, N.Y.: Barron's Educational Series, 1999), 45.

4. Dan Schaefer and Christine Lyons, *How Do We Tell the Children? A Parents' Guide to Helping Children Understand and Cope When Someone Dies* (New York: Newmarket Press, 1986), 33-4.

5. J. William Worden, *Children and Grief: When a Parent Dies* (New York: Guilford Press, 1996), 33-4.

6. James A. Fogarty, *The Magical Thoughts of Grieving Children: Treating Children with Complicated Mourning and Advice for Parents* (Amityville, N.Y.: Baywood, 2000), 160, adapted.

7. Therese A. Rando, *Grieving: How to Go on Living When Someone You Love Dies* (Lexington, Mass.: Lexington Books, 1988), 218.

8. Schaefer and Lyons, *How Do We Tell the Children?* 142.

9. Linda Jane Vogel, *Helping a Child Understand Death* (Philadelphia: Fortress, 1975), 63-4.

Chapter 9: Feel Their Feelings Too

1. Dan Schaefer and Christine Lyons, *How Do We Tell the Children? A Parents' Guide to Helping Children Understand and Cope When Someone Dies* (New York: Newmarket Press, 1986), 29.

2. Archibald D. Hart, *Stress and Your Child* (Waco: Word, 1992), 224.

3. Joseph Braga and Laurie Braga, *Children and Adults: Activities for Growing Together* (Englewood Cliffs, N.J.: Prentice-Hall, 1976), 262-4, adapted.

4. Alan D. Wolfelt, *Healing the Bereaved Child: Grief Gardening, Growth Through Grief, and Other Touchstones for Caregivers* (Fort Collins, Colo.: Compassion Press, 1996), 88-90, adapted.

5. Claudia Jewett Jarrett, *Helping Children Cope with Separation and Loss* (Boston: Harvard Common Press, 1982), 113, adapted.

6. Louise Desport, "1946 Desperate Fables," *American Journal of Orthopsychiatry* (January 16): 100-3.

Chapter 10: Help Them Get Unstuck

1. Alan D. Wolfelt, *Healing the Bereaved Child* (Fort Collins, Colo.: Companion Press, 2001), 313, adapted.

2. Wolfelt, *Healing the Bereaved Child,* 70-2, adapted.

3. Carol Staudacher, *Beyond Grief: A Guide for Recovering from the Death of a Loved One* (Oakland, Calif.: New Harbinger, 1987), 146-7.

4. Staudacher, *Beyond Grief,* 151.

5. Sharon Marshall with Jeff Johnson, *Take My Hand: Guiding Your Child Through Grief* (Grand Rapids, Mich.: Zondervan, 2001), 22-3.

6. Claudia Jewett Jarrett, *Helping Children Cope with Separation and Loss* (Boston: Harvard Common Press, 1982), 85-6.

7. Maria Trozzi with Kathy Massimini, *Talking with Children About Loss: Words, Strategies, and Wisdom to Help Children Cope with Death, Divorce, and Other Difficult Times* (New York: Perigee, 1999), 39.

Chapter 11: Depression: When Feelings Get "Stuffed"

1. Brent Q. Hafen and Brenda Peterson with Kathryn Frandsen, *The Crisis Intervention Handbook* (Englewood Cliffs, N.J.: Prentice-Hall, 1982), 21-39, adapted.

2. Archibald D. Hart, *Unlocking the Mystery of Your Emotions* (Dallas: Word, 1989), 80-2.

3. William Lee Carter, *KidThink* (Dallas: Word, Rapha, 1992), 129, adapted.

4. Carter, *Kid Think,* 142.

5. Frederic F. Flach and Suzanne C. Draghi, *The Nature and Treatment of Depression* (New York: Wiley and Sons, 1975), 89-90, adapted.

6. Carter, *Kid Think,* 134-5.

7. Debra Whiting Alexander, *Children Changed by Trauma: A Healing Guide* (Oakland, Calif.: New Harbinger, 1999), 6-7, adapted.

8. Carter, *Kid Think,* 136.

9. Madeleine L'Engle, *Two-part Invention: The Story of a Marriage* (New York: Farrar, Straus & Giroux, 1988), 124.

Chapter 12: Divorce: A Never-Ending Grief

1. Judith S. Wallerstein, Julia M. Lewis, and Sandra Blakeslee, *The Unexpected Legacy of Divorce: A 25 Year Landmark Study* (New York: Hyperion, 2000), xxvii, 299.

2. Edward Teyber, *Helping Children Cope with Divorce* (San Francisco: Jossey-Bass, 2001), 109, adapted.

3. Jonathan Sandoval, ed., *Handbook of Crisis Counseling, Intervention, and Prevention in the Schools* (Mahwah, N.J.: Lawrence Erlbaum Associates, 2001), 91.

4. Teyber, *Helping Children Cope,* 68ff, adapted.

5. Teyber, *Helping Children Cope,* 13-4, adapted.

6. Archibald D. Hart, *Children and Divorce: What to Expect, How to Help* (Waco: Word, 1982), 66-74.

Chapter 13: Trauma: It Shouldn't Happen to a Child

1. Wendy N. Zubenko and Joseph Capozzoli, eds., *Children and Disasters: A Practical Guide to Healing and Recovery* (New York: Oxford University Press, 2002), 99, adapted.

2. Robin Karr-Morse and Meredith S. Wiley, *Ghosts from the Nursery: Tracing the Roots of Violence* (New York: Atlantic Monthly Press, 1997), 159, 163, adapted.

3. Kendall Johnson, *Trauma in the Lives of Children* (Alameda, Calif.: Hunter House, 1998), 46-7, adapted.

4. Johnson, *Trauma,* 63, adapted.

5. Johnson, *Trauma,* 67-72, adapted.

6. Johnson, *Trauma,* 99, adapted.

7. Johnson, *Trauma,* 99-100, adapted.

8. Debra Whiting Alexander, *Children Changed by Trauma: A Healing Guide* (Oakland, Calif.: New Harbinger, 1999), 81-2, adapted.

9. Alexander, *Children Changed,* 6, adapted.

10. Zubenko, *Children and Disasters,* 96-7.

Appendix A: Remembering Grandparents

1. Maria Trozzi with Kathy Massimini, *Talking with Children About Loss: Words, Strategies, and Wisdom to Help Children Cope with Death, Divorce, and Other Difficult Times* (New York: Perigee, 1999), 13.

Appendix B: Helping Children Tell Their Traumatic Story

1. Debra Whiting Alexander, *Children Changed by Trauma: A Healing Guide* (Oakland, Calif.: New Harbinger, 1999), 25-6.

About the Author

H. Norman Wright is a licensed Marriage, Family, and Child Therapist. He was formerly the director of the Graduate Department of Marriage, Family, and Child Counseling at Biola University, as well as an associate professor of psychology. He was also an associate professor of Christian education and the director of the Graduate Department of Christian Education at the Talbot School of Theology. At the present time he is Research Professor of Christian Education at this institution. He was in private practice for over thirty years.

Dr. Wright is a graduate of Westmont College, Fuller Theological Seminary (MRE), and Pepperdine University (MA). He has received two honorary doctorates, DD and DLit, from Western Conservative Baptist Seminary and Biola University respectively.

He is the author of more than seventy books, including *Always Daddy's Girl, Experiencing Grief, The New Guide to Crisis and Trauma Counseling, Recovering from the Losses of Life, Quiet Times for Couples,* and *Before You Say "I Do."* Dr. Wright has pioneered premarital counseling programs throughout the country. He conducts seminars on parenting, recovering from the losses of life, trauma and crisis counseling, and marriage enrichment.

His current focus is on crisis and trauma counseling and critical-incident debriefings. Part of his work is developing curriculum on loss, crisis, and trauma, as well as community-wide grief recovery seminars. He is a certified Trauma Specialist.

He and his wife, Joyce, have been married for forty-four years and live in Bakersfield, California.

If you would like further information regarding H. Norman Wright, please visit the Web site www.hnormanwright.com or call 1-800-875-7560.